SCIENCE TRICKS AND MAGIC FOR YOUNG PEOPLE

by George Barr

Illustrated by Mildred Waltrip

Dover Publications, Inc.
New York

This Dover edition, first published in 1987, is an unabridged republication of the work first published in 1968 by the McGraw-Hill Book Company, New York under the title, *Fun and Tricks for Young Scientists.*

Manufactured in the United States of America
Dover Publications, Inc., 31 East 2nd Street, Mineola, N.Y. 11501

Library of Congress Cataloging-in-Publication Data

Barr, George, 1907–
  Science tricks and magic for young people.

  Reprint. Originally published: Fun and tricks for young scientists. New York : McGraw-Hill, 1968.
  Includes index.
  Summary: Explains how to perform over twenty-five tricks, oddities, and effects, based on scientific principles, including "Fun with a Clotheshanger," "Catching Air in a Paper Bag," and "Walking Through a Calling Card."
  1. Scientific recreations—Juvenile literature. [1. Scientific recreations] I. Waltrip, Mildred, ill. II. Title.

Q164.B33 1987   793.8   87-9193
ISBN 0-486-25453-4 (pbk.)

Preface

I toyed with the idea of sentimentally calling this fun book *Memoirs of a Young Scientist,* because it is an unforgettable collection of tricks and clever oddities which delighted me over half a century ago when I was an eager, wide-eyed experimenter.

I recall the warm glow of pleasure I felt whenever I was able to astonish my family and friends with these unusual effects. I am certain that the stunts also helped make my thirty-five years of science teaching more enjoyable for me, as well as for my students. Even during my days as a professional magician, my routines always contained science tricks, for they elicited startling and humorous reactions from the audience.

Science is curious and unbelievable at times, but it is always fascinating, especially when one knows the reasons behind some mysterious demonstration. That is why every trick in this book is explained in simple terms.

In a science show, unlike a magic performance, it is a kind and friendly gesture to tell the audience the explanation—but you don't have to do this immediately. Let the people give their own reasons first. This is part of the fun, since some answers may be funnier than the trick! Then, when the ideas are exhausted, the performer can dramatically reveal the trick to his appreciative listeners.

George Barr

Contents

Introduction

There are very few completely new tricks in science. Some may appear brand-new to you because you may never have seen them before, or perhaps they have been given a new twist so that you do not recognize them.

In this recreational book you are encouraged to invent new devices and to experiment with novel approaches. In this way, even an old trick can be made to reflect your own inimitable personality and style. The description of some tricks may seem rather lengthy, but that is because suggestions are often given for alternate, modified methods of building, as well as demonstrating the devices.

Certain sections are written so that the patter and showmanship are built into the instructions. It is impossible to do this for all the tricks, but you should be able to get an idea of what to do for other presentations.

Each trick has been carefully tested. Stunts which are delicate or temperamental, and work only part of the time, have been methodically discarded. The use of simple tools is suggested throughout the book. As a young experimenter you should own a few common, everyday tools. Learn to use them safely and skillfully. Reserve an area in your home as your workshop.

This "fun and tricks" book covers many areas of science. You will be working with electricity, air pressure, liquids, chemicals, light, heat, motion, mathematics, and much more. No dangerous effects are included and all devices are easily constructed. All materials are readily available and inexpensive.

Many activities may not seem to be about science. However, they have been included because of their novelty and curiosity. Scientists are greatly intrigued and amused by stunts calling for use of the imagination and visualization. Even riddles, puzzles, jokes, and just plain magic tricks are sprinkled in here and there, just to keep your friends guessing and alert. Some should keep your leisure time busily occupied for many hours. You may wish to present some of the tricks at parties, assembly shows, clubs, or science fairs.

Here are a few examples of the science tricks you will learn to do in this book:

Build a simple electric-light circuit. But when the switch is *on*, the light goes *off!* When the switch is open the light goes on. Crazy and baffling!

Catch a handful of air "thrown" into a paper bag with a loud, realistic thud.

Lay half a rubber ball on the floor. At your command it will leap high into the air.

10

Actually make your mother or sister lose weight immediately without dieting.

Make a penny cling upside-down to the tip of a clotheshanger hook as it is being twirled around a finger. Magically suspend ping-pong balls in midair. Design a motor which is activated by air from a vacuum cleaner. Command divers to go up or down in a bottle of water.

Let a friend huff on a mirror to prove that he is alive—and watch his own name appear on the fogged glass!

Prepare secret messages with a clever device which the F.B.I. would have trouble deciphering.

Make colorful, whirling scientific toys to place around the house. Show how you "dissolve" a coin in water. Build a meter to show that when rubber is heated it will contract instead of expanding.

Do number tricks with real magical endings. Tell the numbers on a dollar bill in someone's wallet. Or call a name picked from the telephone book to verify your prediction.

Make a five-pointed star, or a cross, from a folded piece of paper with just one snip of the scissors.

Design a simple peg that can fit into circular holes—and into square and triangular ones as well.

Do you feel yourself getting impatient and more and more curious? Then this book is for you. Go to it!

1

BALANCE A COIN ON
THE HOOK OF YOUR BENT
CLOTHES HANGER, AND
SLOWLY BEGIN TO SPIN IT
AROUND YOUR FINGER.
COIN WILL STAY IN PLACE.

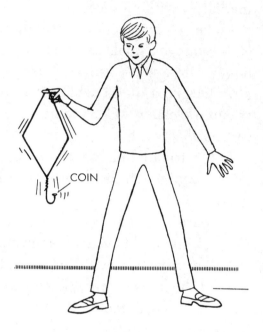

COIN

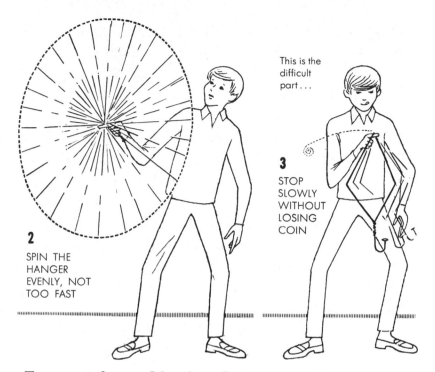

This is the
difficult
part . . .

2
SPIN THE
HANGER
EVENLY, NOT
TOO FAST

3
STOP
SLOWLY
WITHOUT
LOSING
COIN

Fun with a Clotheshanger

You can have a barrel of scientific fun with a group of your friends using just an ordinary wire clotheshanger and a penny. You merely ask for a clotheshanger, pull it slightly out of shape, and balance a penny upon the tip of the hook. Then proceed to spin the hanger, with the balanced coin, in a circle around your index (pointing) finger. Even when you stop spinning, the coin will not fall off its delicate perch. Soon everyone is trying to repeat your performance, but with little success.

To prepare the hanger, hold the hook in one hand and pull the middle of the bottom wire in a direction

13

away from the hook. This will form an angle in the wire so that the hanger becomes elongated.

Suspend the bent hanger so that the angle you have formed is over your index finger and the hook part is down, as shown in the illustration. If necessary, bend the hook so that the balanced coin can be *balanced horizontally* on the tip. Your friends may think that just keeping the penny balanced on a non-moving hanger tip is a feat. But when you start swinging the hanger and the coin around your finger, everyone will be amazed when the delicately balanced coin still does not fall off the hook. Bring the spinning hanger to a halt and the coin remains on its tiny post as though it were glued.

After you have successfully demonstrated this trick, ask others to duplicate it. Of course, they rarely can do so because it takes a little know-how.

In fact, the first few times you attempt this trick you will probably not succeed either. But after a little practice you will find that you can consistently keep the coin on the hook during your spinning and stopping.

While this trick works with almost every wire hanger, it is best to select one which already has a somewhat flattened tip. Or, for extra insurance, you might file the tip flat. It might also help to have all the wire in the pulled-out hanger in one plane. To do this, lay the prepared hanger on a table. Then, if necessary, bend certain sections so that every part of the hanger touches the flat table.

Try the trick with nickels, dimes, quarters, and even half-dollars. Do not make fast starts or stops. If you do, you will be fighting inertia. Inertia is the tendency of an object to continue doing what it is already doing. If the object is at rest, it will tend to remain at rest even when a force starts moving it. If the object is moving, it will tend to continue moving, even if a force is stopping it. If you start too quickly, the coin's inertia will cause it to be left behind, and it will fall off its delicate perch. Once the penny and the hook are moving at the same speed, you must not stop suddenly, because the coin's inertia will cause it to continue moving, and it will fly off its perch.

Besides inertia, there is another reason why the coin does not fly off as everyone expects. To keep an object moving in a circle, you must continually exert a force pulling it toward the center of the circle. This force is called CENTRIPETAL FORCE. This inward push is what is pressing the hanger tip against the balanced coin. Friction also helps keep the coin in place.

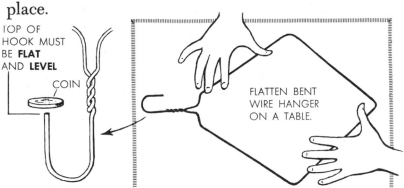

TOP OF
HOOK MUST
BE **FLAT**
AND **LEVEL**

COIN

FLATTEN BENT
WIRE HANGER
ON A TABLE.

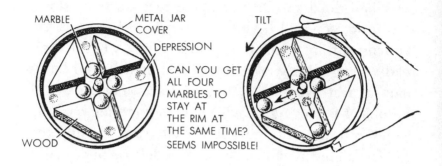

MARBLE METAL JAR COVER TILT

DEPRESSION

CAN YOU GET ALL FOUR MARBLES TO STAY AT THE RIM AT THE SAME TIME? SEEMS IMPOSSIBLE!

WOOD

Centrifugal Puzzle

This novel scientific trick is remarkably easy to perform—once the secret is known. But most of your friends will probably bite their nails down to their knuckles in exasperation trying to solve the puzzle.

The setup is made from a large, metal, screw-top cover, such as those found on glass containers. The cover has four marbles in it, each one in a guided runway from the center to the rim. At the start, each marble sits in its own depression and touches a center post. The trick is to get all four marbles to move to other depressions at the rim and remain there *at the same time.*

This is impossible until the cover is given a spin while it is on a level surface. The four marbles will now roll away from the center. When the spinning ceases, the marbles are all in place at the rim. The tendency of materials to move away from the center of a spinning object is called the CENTRIFUGAL EFFECT.

16

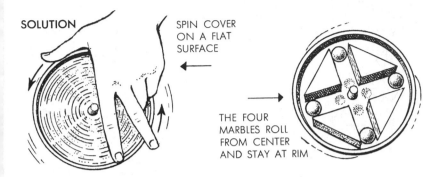

SOLUTION

SPIN COVER
ON A FLAT
SURFACE

←

→

THE FOUR
MARBLES ROLL
FROM CENTER
AND STAY AT RIM

Obtain a large cover about 3½ inches or more in diameter. The size found on large jars of coffee is suitable. You may remove the inside paper seal or leave it in place. Mark the center of the cover.

Find four glass marbles about ⁹⁄₁₆ inch in diameter. If you do not have these at home, you may use four large, perfectly round beads, made of wood or some other material. Large, steel ball bearings would be excellent. You have lots of leeway as to the size of any of the above items, but do not use anything much larger than the size suggested for the marbles.

To measure the runways for the marbles, proceed as follows. First, use a pencil to trace the circle made by the cover on a sheet of paper. Mark the center with a dot. Now rule two parallel lines on each side of this center point. Your marble or bead should be able to move freely between the lines.

Make a similar set of double lines through the center at right angles to the first set. Draw a line be-

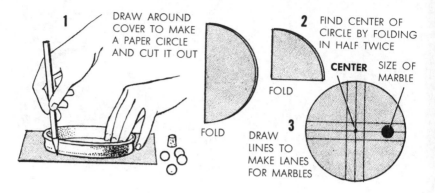

1 DRAW AROUND COVER TO MAKE A PAPER CIRCLE AND CUT IT OUT

FOLD

FOLD

2 FIND CENTER OF CIRCLE BY FOLDING IN HALF TWICE

CENTER   SIZE OF MARBLE

3 DRAW LINES TO MAKE LANES FOR MARBLES

tween the points where the crossing lines touch the edge of the circle. This forms a triangle between the runways. As you can see in the illustration, you have now laid out the triangles which form the runways.

Cut out one triangle and use it as a pattern for making four wooden or cardboard triangles. It is not necessary to have the triangle right up against the circumference. Cut your pattern so that you have ⅛-inch clearance. This will allow easier adjustment of the finished triangles. Here is another hint: you can get a triangle with just one cut by laying your pattern on the squared corner of a piece of wood.

You can make the runway guides from soft wood about ½ inch thick. Balsa wood is very easy to use; even a razor blade cuts it. If you wish, you may use heavy cardboard cut into triangles. Glue layer after layer together until you have the required height. Make sure the sides which will serve as runway guides are smooth and vertical.

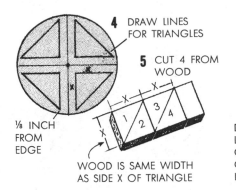

4 DRAW LINES FOR TRIANGLES

5 CUT 4 FROM WOOD

⅛ INCH FROM EDGE

WOOD IS SAME WIDTH AS SIDE X OF TRIANGLE

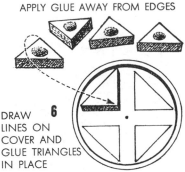

APPLY GLUE AWAY FROM EDGES

6 DRAW LINES ON COVER AND GLUE TRIANGLES IN PLACE

Carefully lay out the four finished wood or cardboard triangles in the jar cover to form four runways. Leave plenty of clearance for the marbles to move. Make pencil outlines on the cover for reference.

Glue each triangle in the place which you marked for it. Use airplane-model glue or similar fast-drying adhesive. Duco cement is excellent, too. You can do a neat job by not applying the glue too heavily near the front edges so that it will squeeze out onto the runway. It is not easy to remove certain glues. However, you may apply a heavy amount of glue under the base of the triangle. Excess glue here would not ooze out onto the marble runways.

Make the final adjustments of the triangles before the glue starts to set. Now glue a small cork over the center point. Wood or rubber pegs may also be used and must be large enough to prevent the balls from rolling out of the runways. Let the glue dry thoroughly.

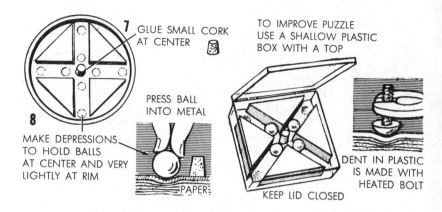

7 GLUE SMALL CORK AT CENTER

PRESS BALL INTO METAL

MAKE DEPRESSIONS TO HOLD BALLS AT CENTER AND VERY LIGHTLY AT RIM

8

PAPER

TO IMPROVE PUZZLE USE A SHALLOW PLASTIC BOX WITH A TOP

KEEP LID CLOSED

DENT IN PLASTIC IS MADE WITH HEATED BOLT

You must now make a depression or slight cup for each ball to rest in when it is touching the center stop. These indentations are very important, since they prevent the balls from rolling until the cover is given a pronounced slant. Without these holes, all four balls might accidentally roll into the depressions at the other end of the runway.

To make a depression at the center, place the cover on several thicknesses of newspaper. Move your marble, or whatever ball you are using, up to the center stop. Now press down hard on the marble. Notice that it has left a dent in the soft cover. Repeat the pressing, placing a book over the marble. If you still cannot get a good depression, try standing on the book. Or you might give it a blow with a hammer. Usually, pressing with one's fingers is sufficient.

Make depressions for each of the four marbles touching the center stop.

Now make *slight* depressions with each marble at the rim in the runway. *Press very, very slightly* on the marble with your fingers. Spin the puzzle, and if a marble does not remain at the rim, then make the depression very slightly deeper. If the four depressions near the rim were quite deep, then anybody could strike the cover so that the marbles would bounce out of the center holes. They would find their way into the holes at the end of the runway and stay there.

If by accident you made an end hole too deep, you can decrease the depression. Just pinch the marble, press down, and rub it back and forth over the dent.

Make a few puzzles so you can have several people working on them at one time. If you wish to have the cover spin longer, you can press a dimple into the cover from the center point. This will act as a pivot.

You can have a covered puzzle so that the marbles cannot be removed. Make it from a plastic box. Find a small, shallow, round or square container of clear plastic. Dime stores often sell such empty "storage" boxes. Depressions can be made by banging the marbles on the plastic or by using heated metal bars or bolts. Hold a bolt with pliers over the kitchen range. When the metal gets warm (not red hot), press it over the plastic. It should leave a dent.

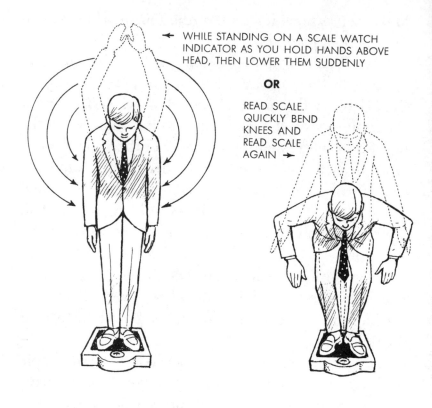

WHILE STANDING ON A SCALE WATCH INDICATOR AS YOU HOLD HANDS ABOVE HEAD, THEN LOWER THEM SUDDENLY

OR

READ SCALE. QUICKLY BEND KNEES AND READ SCALE AGAIN →

A Very Quick Way to Lose Weight

Can you think of the fastest method of losing weight without going on a starvation diet? Of course, you could take a rocket to the moon where the pull of gravity is less than on earth, and then the scale would show less weight. But if you do not wish to leave home right now, you can get on a bathroom or other type of scale with your arms raised above your head. Notice your weight on the dial.

22

Now suddenly bring your arms down to your sides. The scale will show quite a loss in weight for an instant, then return to normal. This probably fooled you, because you thought your weight would increase as you brought your arms down.

This effect is based on Sir Isaac Newton's law of reaction: every action has an equal but opposite reaction. Bringing the arms down produced an upward action on your body by the scale's platform. This lessened your weight.

Another way of losing weight is to stand on the scale and simply bend your knees. This brings your body down, while the scale's reaction is upward, lessening the weight.

Try this on your lady relatives who are probably always on a reducing diet. It is too bad that this method is not permanent!

To suddenly gain weight, raise your arms quickly. This action produces a downward reaction on the scale, and your weight momentarily increases.

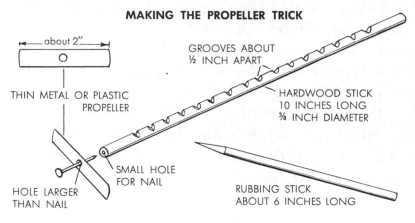

about 2″

THIN METAL OR PLASTIC PROPELLER

GROOVES ABOUT ½ INCH APART

HARDWOOD STICK 10 INCHES LONG ⅜ INCH DIAMETER

HOLE LARGER THAN NAIL

SMALL HOLE FOR NAIL

RUBBING STICK ABOUT 6 INCHES LONG

The Obedient Propeller

Here is another "Do as I do" stunt which you can demonstrate with disdainful ease. But when others attempt to imitate your success, they howl with frustration and usually give up in disgust.

The device is easily constructed and consists of a notched stick with a loose-fitting propeller at one end. The opposite end is held in one hand while the other hand rubs a hardwood stick (about 6 inches long) or a pencil back and forth over the notches.

Wonders of wonders! The propeller mysteriously starts turning and gathers speed. On command, the propeller obediently comes to a halt and even reverses its direction of rotation. All this time, the rubbing continues back and forth. The problem for your friends is to discover how to make the propeller turn at all—and also how to reverse its direction of rotation.

The notched stick is 10 inches long and should be made of hardwood. A birch or maple dowel or flagstick about ⅜ inch in diameter is excellent. However, if available, square strips may also be used.

The notches are about ⅛ inch deep and can be cut by a file, knife, or saw; they should be about ½ inch apart. Leave about 1 inch from either end of the stick unnotched.

The propeller is a flat piece of thin metal or a strip from a *thin* plastic ruler, about 2 inches long and ½ inch wide.

Obtain a short, thin nail with a head on it. Use a drill to make a smooth hole in the center of the metal. A leather hole-puncher can be used for the thin plastic propeller. In either case, it is important that the hole should be about twice as large as the thickness of the nail.

Place the nail through the propeller and drive it straight (without a slant) into the center of the end of the notched stick. Be careful not to split the wood. If possible, drill a hole smaller than the nail before driving the nail. There is no need to twist the metal into the customary propeller shape, but it should be evenly balanced by carefully trimming the longer end with scissors or a file.

To operate this maddening gadget, grasp the end of the notched stick in one hand. Rub the notches with the stick or pencil held in the other hand. Vary your method of rubbing while watching the propeller closely. When the propeller starts to spin, no matter how feebly, continue doing what you believe is causing the spinning.

Experiment by increasing or decreasing the pressure or by rubbing different portions of the stick. You may discover that the most effective changes are brought about by pressing against the notched stick with the thumb and index finger which are holding the rubbing stick. In a short time you will be the master of the situation.

To reverse the motion of the propeller while continuing the rubbing, simply find the correct positions of the thumb and index finger pressing against the notched stick. It is interesting that what works for one person will not get the same results for another.

Can you guess how a back-and-forth movement makes the propeller go around in a circle? Many of your unscientific friends will say the cause is static electricity. Of course they are wrong. Here is the explanation.

Rubbing the notches does not make the stick vibrate only up and down. Instead, the nail end of the propeller stick acquires a circular vibration. This is due to the fact that the finger muscles and bones are holding the notched stick in a swivel or all-directional hinge. The pressure of the thumb on the rubbing stick also helps produce a circular series of jerks in one direction of rotation. Changing this position causes a series of jolts in an opposite circular direction.

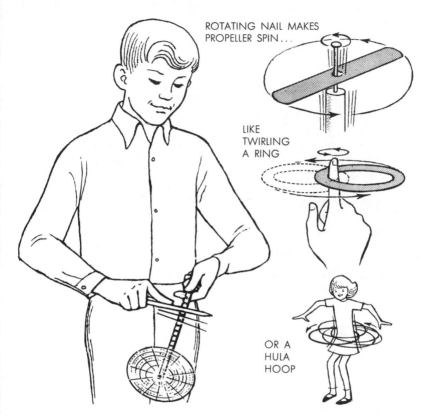

ROTATING NAIL MAKES
PROPELLER SPIN...

LIKE
TWIRLING
A RING

OR A
HULA
HOOP

The impacts of the thin nail against the oversized circular hole in the propeller gives it the spinning motion. You can demonstrate this by twirling your finger inside a hoop or inside a circle cut in a piece of cardboard.

Use showmanship with this trick. Pretend to talk to the propeller, commanding it to change directions. Do not be too quick to tell your friends how to operate the propeller. Let them find out the hard way—the way you did!

The Frisky Handball

This amusing trick never fails to command everyone's attention because it produces unexpected action and noise. One half of a broken ball is placed on the floor, and after a certain known interval it suddenly leaps into the air with a loud bang.

You will need an old, small black rubber handball.

You are familiar with this rather hard handball having a diameter of 1⅞ inches. Try to obtain one which has lost its bounce and is therefore useless as a handball. It is still good for this stunt. Ask your friends for such a ball.

If you have difficulty getting one, you may try some other ball like it, one which is made of thick rubber. However, the regulation handball is best for this trick, since its rubber is about ¼ inch thick.

Notice that the ball has a light seam dividing it into two equal halves. If you cannot see this line, then make your own division line with a sharp pencil.

Cut the ball into two parts along the seam. This is usually easy once the cut is started. You can often just squeeze the ball and it will tear itself in two. Start the cut carefully with a coping saw or knife, if possible in a vise.

Turn the half-ball inside out. Place the inverted ball on any hard floor, not a rug. The inside of the ball is now facing up. After a short pause, during which the ball is slowly inverting itself, it will suddenly snap and leap upward with a very loud pop.

Do this again for a few times until you know at what count the jump occurs after you lay down the ball. When you perform this trick put the inverted ball down on the floor or table. Start counting, and when you come to the correct number, point your index finger like a gun at the ball and say "Bang-bang-bang!" Another effect is to place the triggered ball

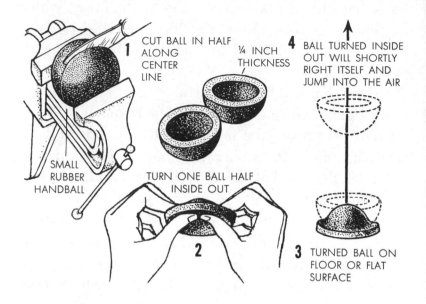

1 CUT BALL IN HALF ALONG CENTER LINE

¼ INCH THICKNESS

SMALL RUBBER HANDBALL

TURN ONE BALL HALF INSIDE OUT

2

4 BALL TURNED INSIDE OUT WILL SHORTLY RIGHT ITSELF AND JUMP INTO THE AIR

3 TURNED BALL ON FLOOR OR FLAT SURFACE

into a friend's palm. Ask him to cup the other hand over the ball. When the ball snaps, the person's hand gets a rude spanking.

In order for this trick to work, the half-ball must be a certain size. If it is too short, it will leap up too fast, almost as soon as you put it down. If the ball is too large, it will not invert itself at all.

Usually, one of the two halves of the cut ball is ideal for this trick. But if both do not work because one is too large and the other too small, do not despair. There are cures for each one of these conditions.

You can make the large hemisphere smaller so that it will jump up faster. Proceed as follows. Place a

30

TO MAKE BALL
SMALLER FOR
FASTER TURNING

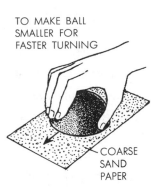

COARSE
SAND
PAPER

TO MAKE BALL JUMP
MORE QUICKLY PINCH
AND TIE IT TOGETHER
RIGHT SIDE OUT

TO JUMP **MORE SLOWLY**
PINCH BALL AND TIE IT
TOGETHER **INSIDE OUT**

LEAVE IT TIED OVERNIGHT

large sheet of coarse sandpaper on a flat surface. Set the half-ball on it, with the cut side down, and rub it against the sandpaper until it is the correct size.

You will find it easier to do this if you rub in only one direction. Keep turning the ball after each rubbing stroke across the sandpaper. Test often until the ball inverts itself at about the count of six.

There is another way to make the ball jump up faster, without sandpapering off any rubber. Simply squeeze the ball together in a vise overnight, or squeeze the ball and keep it tied in this position for a day or so until the rubber adjusts itself.

If the half-ball jumps up too fast, you must turn it inside out, pinch the edges together, and place it in a vise or tie it with string in this squeezed position. After a day or so, test it again.

If at any time the inverted ball does not jump up at all, you can still get an interesting effect by lightly

31

tapping the sole of your shoe on the dome of the ball while it is on the floor. It will always upset itself and jump up against your shoe with a real firecracker pop.

This entertaining trick works, since the thick rubber will come back to its original position because of its elasticity. The rubber starts changing shape slowly, but near the end there is a sudden movement as the dome pops out.

You know that every action has an equal and opposite reaction. The action of the dome sharply striking *down* against the floor causes the floor to react *upward* against the ball and send it high into the air.

Hilarious Party Race

Funny contests are always in order at a party. Here is one especially designed for science-minded contestants. Players are told to clasp their hands behind their backs. On the table before them are placed similar bottles or glasses of soda, water, or any other beverage. Each person now gets two drinking straws thrust between the lips. The first one who drinks all the liquid gets the prize.

Tell them to start the race when you count to three. Start counting, but after number two pause and pretend that you had an afterthought—a mighty brainstorm. Announce that the rules are that a player must keep only one straw in the liquid. The other straw should always be *outside* the bottle or glass.

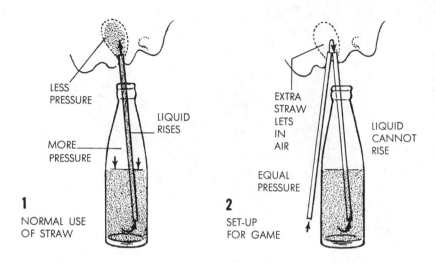

LESS
PRESSURE

MORE
PRESSURE

LIQUID
RISES

1

NORMAL USE
OF STRAW

EXTRA
STRAW
LETS
IN
AIR

EQUAL
PRESSURE

LIQUID
CANNOT
RISE

2

SET-UP
FOR GAME

When the race begins, each opponent will suddenly discover that it is impossible to use drinking straws in this way. Liquid goes up a straw because a person, without thinking about it, lessens the air pressure inside the mouth which is tightly sealed around the straw.

But the air pressure on the surface of the liquid in the bottle or glass has not changed. It is now greater than on the liquid inside the straw. Obviously, when there are unbalanced forces, there will be a movement toward the lesser force. That is why the liquid goes up into the mouth. It is really not "sucked" up, it is pushed up.

The above explanation gives away the secret of how to win at this game. The straw which is not in the glass, being open to the outside air, does not allow the pressure in the mouth to be decreased. A

34

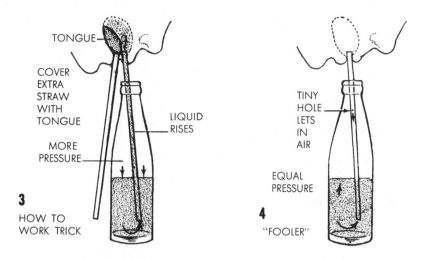

TONGUE

COVER
EXTRA
STRAW
WITH
TONGUE

MORE
PRESSURE

3

HOW TO
WORK TRICK

LIQUID
RISES

TINY
HOLE
LETS
IN
AIR

EQUAL
PRESSURE

4

"FOOLER"

smart player will place his tongue tightly over the end of the open straw which is in his mouth. This is not easy to do without hands.

There is a very humorous follow-up to this stunt. First, build up the winner with flowery complements and much fanfare. Praise the knowledge and quick thinking which made success possible. Then announce, "Now that everyone knows the science principle behind this trick, how about a rematch? Let's have another similar race!"

This time give a former, and cocky winner, a straw which you have secretly prepared by making a tiny pinhole about 2 inches from the top. This will be unnoticeable. See that this straw is the one placed inside the liquid. Then watch the expression of utter disbelief on the face of the frustrated player. What a let-down!

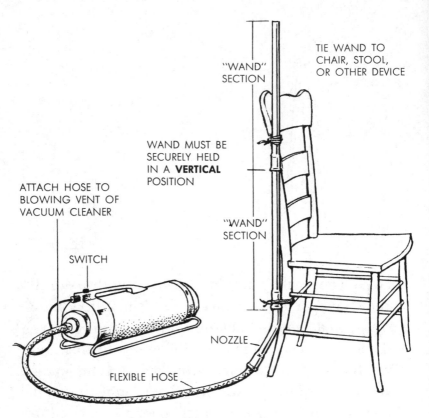

"WAND" SECTION

TIE WAND TO CHAIR, STOOL, OR OTHER DEVICE

WAND MUST BE SECURELY HELD IN A **VERTICAL** POSITION

ATTACH HOSE TO BLOWING VENT OF VACUUM CLEANER

SWITCH

"WAND" SECTION

NOZZLE

FLEXIBLE HOSE

Merrymaking with a Vacuum Cleaner

You can have good clean scientific fun with any household vacuum cleaner which has a hose attachment for blowing air. Your mother need not worry, because you are not going to harm the device in any way. You are going to use it only as a blower.

Tell her that your materials will not even scratch the metal or paint. You will also be mindful not to overheat the motor by running it for unusually long periods or by blocking the exit of the air. In fact, after she sees the first stunt, and hears your explanation, she will be so delighted she will invite her neighbors in to see her young scientist's work.

Demonstrating "Anti-Gravity"

The steel air-tube attachments of your vacuum cleaner are called WANDS. This is an appropriate name, because you are going to do feats of scientific magic with them. Fit two tubes together so that you get a long extension. Slip the end over the nozzle of the flexible rubber hose which you have attached to the *blowing* vent of the machine.

Secure the long wand in a vertical position. You might tie it to a chair with a straight back, or devise some other method. Step back and look at the wand. Make necessary adjustments to get the tube in the most vertical position possible.

Blow up a large *round* balloon and wrap a rubber band tightly around the neck. Start the motor and place the inflated balloon in the center of the air stream, a few feet above the end of the vertical tube. Of course, everyone will expect the balloon to be blown away. Instead, it remains mysteriously suspended in the gale of rushing air!

You will discover the best position after a few trials. Prevent a cross-draft from an open window or door or another fan. Do not try this stunt too close to

37

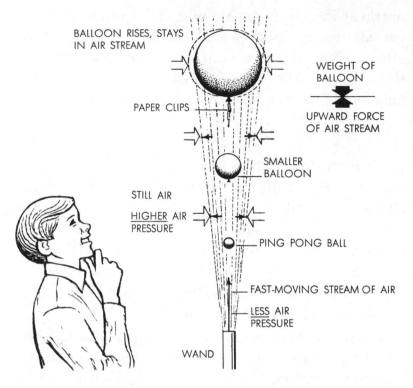

BALLOON RISES, STAYS IN AIR STREAM

WEIGHT OF BALLOON

PAPER CLIPS

UPWARD FORCE OF AIR STREAM

SMALLER BALLOON

STILL AIR

HIGHER AIR PRESSURE

PING PONG BALL

FAST-MOVING STREAM OF AIR

LESS AIR PRESSURE

WAND

a wall or a very low ceiling which may reflect the blowing air.

The balloon may swing back and forth, yet it will remain in the air stream. This adds to the fun and excitement. But sometimes it may get too wild and escape. If you wish to keep it steadier, you must weigh it down by attaching paper clips or other weights to the neck.

This eerie exhibition demonstrates the BERNOULLI EFFECT and is used by scientists to explain various kinds of behavior of liquid streams. (Air is considered a liquid here.) Briefly stated, the Bernoulli effect is this: when the speed of a liquid increases, there is a decrease in pressure.

The fast-moving air coming out of the wand has a lower pressure than the still air around it. Every time the haphazard motion of the balloon brings it to one side, away from the blowing air, the higher pressure outside pushes it back toward the low-pressure area in the fast-moving air. This only explains the side motions. The balloon does not fall because it is supported by the upward force of the rushing air.

Grand Finale

On the stage and in fireworks displays the endings are always showy. You too can build up your "antigravity" act to a spectacular finale. Add various other kinds of round, very lightweight empty spheres to the air stream. A ping-pong ball is excellent. So are other light plastic balls found at toy counters in dime stores.

Inflated round balloons of various sizes will remain suspended at different levels. Use additional balls which will stay away from the other suspended balls. If they strike each other, the momentum will throw one or more out of the air stream.

If you wish, you may walk the entire display around or out of the room. If you are doing this as a stage production, you can march the dancing balls right out into the wings when you make your exit. In the above cases, the wand must be propped up vertically and loosely against your support all the time. The vacuum cleaner's wheels or skids must face the exit so you do not jar the setup.

When ready to walk, grasp the wand and *maintain it vertically* while someone removes the chair or other support. Walk very slowly, avoiding drafts or air reflections. It takes a little careful practice to do this without losing a single ball. However, it is not too difficult if you decide to use few balls. Besides, if several balls or balloons fly out of formation, the audience will howl with glee!

A large funnel taped into the end of the wand often evens out the air flow. So will a piece of cheesecloth tied across the wand outlet. However, with many vacuum cleaners this only cuts down the rate of air flow and makes your demonstration less effective.

Photograph of a Bewitched Ball

Have a careful person take a prize picture of you hypnotizing a ping-pong ball that is suspended in the air with apparently no visible means of support. Of course, the picture must be composed so that it does not show the end of the wand from which the invisible air is blowing. The film will show only your face and hands and the magically hanging ball.

If you wish to sit at a table, you may have a shorter air tube located at the side and just below the level of the tabletop. Hold the fingers of both your hands in

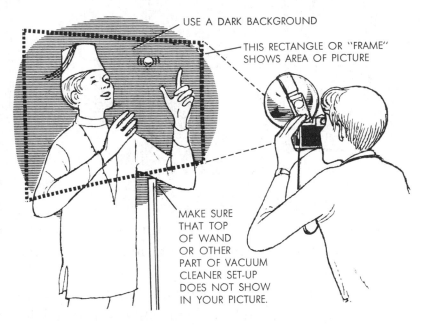

USE A DARK BACKGROUND

THIS RECTANGLE OR "FRAME" SHOWS AREA OF PICTURE

MAKE SURE THAT TOP OF WAND OR OTHER PART OF VACUUM CLEANER SET-UP DOES NOT SHOW IN YOUR PICTURE.

the grasping attitude of a typical spell-casting witch. Or you may hold a ping-pong paddle in one hand to make believe you just struck the ball. Even the experts will wonder how in the world you made such an "action shot."

Take several different pictures. Wear a top hat or a fez like a magician. If nothing else is available, put on a party hat. Hold a magic wand in one hand. Paste a star at the end.

In order to make the white ball stand out, wear something dark. Do not use a distracting background. Have a mysterious, wide-eyed look on your face. Ham it up!

41

A CLEVER WITCH, WITH BALLOONS AND WAND

YOUNG MAGICIAN

PING PONG CHAMP

The picture should be taken at 1/200th of a second or faster. Use a flashbulb, take the exposure near a sunny window, or set up everything outside the house.

Take pains with this photograph and you will have something to be proud of. Do not overlook taking silent moving pictures. They are ideal for this interesting effect. Be especially careful that the movie camera at no time picks up any visible signs of the vacuum cleaner or its tell-tale electric cord.

Magnetic Air Molecules

As a good-natured hoax, you can attempt to explain the suspended balls by means of some scientific double-talk. Do this humorous demonstration. Hold the nozzle of the rubber hose in your hand. Allow several persons to feel the rushing air. It will probably be slightly warm because of the small amount of heat from the motor and also from the friction of the air and the dust and the fan blade.

Glibly say that warm air molecules are like tiny magnets. You will "prove" this by passing the air stream down and over the side of a large balloon suspended from a 2-foot string held by an assistant. The balloon will be suddenly attracted toward the warmed, air blown molecules!

Of course, this is just another example of the Bernoulli effect. So, after a short pause, you must explain this to your friends. It should be a cardinal rule for you never to leave your audience with a wrong explanation of some scientific stunt.

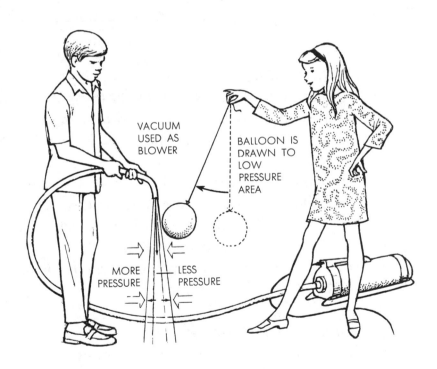

VACUUM USED AS BLOWER

BALLOON IS DRAWN TO LOW PRESSURE AREA

MORE PRESSURE

LESS PRESSURE

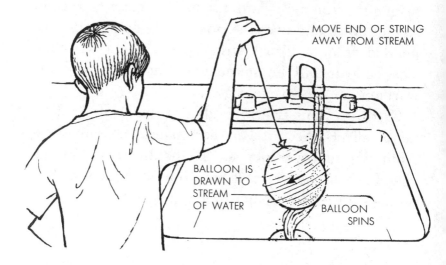

MOVE END OF STRING AWAY FROM STREAM

BALLOON IS DRAWN TO STREAM OF WATER

BALLOON SPINS

Works with Water, Too!

By the way, here is an extra trick to do with the balloon. Hold the end of the string so that the balloon hangs very close to the stream of water coming from a faucet.

Here, too, the balloon is drawn toward the stream. Once the balloon is against the water, draw your hand and the end of the string away from the stream. This produces a more spectacular effect.

Instead of a balloon you may use a spoon, fork, knife, or other item held loosely on top.

The Clinging Ping-Pong Ball

Another Bernoulli demonstration which always surprises people is picking up light round balls or balloons with a jet of blowing air.

44

Insert the stem of a funnel into the end of the wand or nozzle. Tape the area so that no air escapes except through the funnel. Place a ping-pong ball or balloon on the floor. From several feet away show how the blowing air wafts away the light balls. Then carefully place the funnel on top of the ping-pong ball—it gets *drawn up* into the funnel!

A large funnel will pick up a large balloon. The balloon will often rotate like a wheel while it is being held in the funnel. If you do not have a large funnel, use any paper or plastic container with slanted sides, such as the kind used for cottage cheese, sour cream, or other foods in the grocery.

Make a round hole in the bottom. Insert the nozzle into the container about ¼ inch. Tape the car-

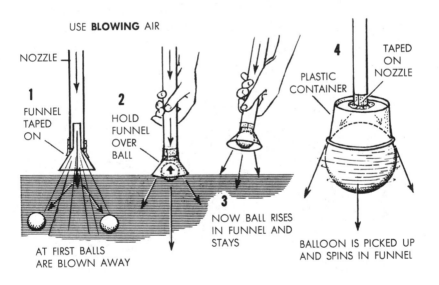

USE **BLOWING** AIR

NOZZLE

1 FUNNEL TAPED ON

2 HOLD FUNNEL OVER BALL

3 NOW BALL RISES IN FUNNEL AND STAYS

AT FIRST BALLS ARE BLOWN AWAY

4 PLASTIC CONTAINER

TAPED ON NOZZLE

BALLOON IS PICKED UP AND SPINS IN FUNNEL

ton to the nozzle with plastic, masking, or adhesive tape.

Bernoulli Again!

Here is still another way to show the reduced pressure of a fast-moving stream of air. Place two large empty, round glass jars or bottles on a hard floor about 2 inches apart and parallel to each other. Hold the vacuum cleaner wand *over* the space between the containers and also parallel to them. This is done to prevent them from being blown away.

Now lower the wand so that the air goes horizontally through the space between the jars or bottles, starting at the end near you.

The glass objects will mysteriously roll together. If not, place them closer together. Always point out that your audience probably expected the rush of air to blow the containers apart—but the opposite effect occurred!

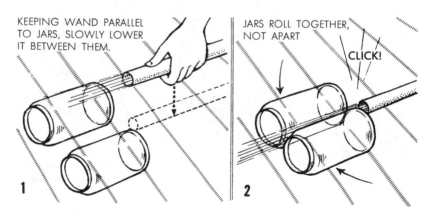

KEEPING WAND PARALLEL TO JARS, SLOWLY LOWER IT BETWEEN THEM.

1

JARS ROLL TOGETHER, NOT APART

CLICK!

2

A Cheery Reaction Motor

Everyone loves a moving gadget. Here is an intriguing one you can build from a large, empty tin can—like a 1-pound coffee container. It is powered by the air blown from your vacuum cleaner, and is capable of rotating on a simple wooden shaft at a merry clip.

The can contains about 36 holes which have been pierced into its surface. The metal around each hole has been twisted by the piercing tool so that the air blown through it moves *toward* the rear. This makes the can move in the opposite direction, just as a jet or rocket moves. One of Newton's laws of motion states that every action produces an equal but opposite reaction, and that is why this whirling device is called a reaction motor.

Many containers which are 5½ inches long have three or more circular grooves running around the can. Use these for marking off the holes, spaced about 1 inch apart. If your can does not have these three depressions, mark off three evenly distributed circles as guide lines.

Use a sharp awl or a large pointed nail to pierce the metal vertically. This is quite easy to do, especially if the sharp pointed tool is moved from side to side while it is being pressed. Try not to bend the can out of shape. For safety's sake, keep the hand which is holding the can out of harm's way should your tool slip.

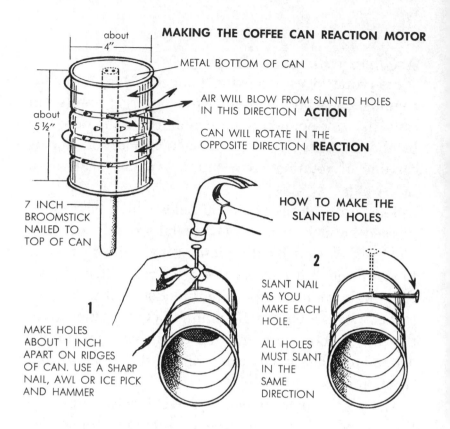

about 4"

METAL BOTTOM OF CAN

AIR WILL BLOW FROM SLANTED HOLES IN THIS DIRECTION **ACTION**

CAN WILL ROTATE IN THE OPPOSITE DIRECTION **REACTION**

about 5½"

7 INCH BROOMSTICK NAILED TO TOP OF CAN

HOW TO MAKE THE SLANTED HOLES

2

SLANT NAIL AS YOU MAKE EACH HOLE.

ALL HOLES MUST SLANT IN THE SAME DIRECTION

1

MAKE HOLES ABOUT 1 INCH APART ON RIDGES OF CAN. USE A SHARP NAIL, AWL OR ICE PICK AND HAMMER

After each hole is pierced, and while the awl or nail is in the hole, slant the tool as far as you can to one side along the circle. This bends the thin metal so that air blown from the inside will be directed toward the rear. Slant all holes in the same direction.

The shaft is a dowel or an old broomstick 7 inches long and about ⅞ inch wide. Nail or screw a flat end to the *exact* center of the inside of the metal bottom of the can.

The bottom of the motor is made from a tight-fitting plastic cover, like those sold with many 1-

pound cans of coffee. This cover is intended to close the coffee can once the can is opened. A very round smooth hole must be made in the center of this cover. It will act as a bearing for the rotating can. It must also serve as a seal to prevent too much air from escaping. It is made in the following way.

Place the cover on the table and set the end of the vacuum-cleaner wand vertically over the center of the cover. Trace the circle made by the end of the wand. Do this with a sharp, dark pencil or ball-point pen. Do this carefully. An off-center hole will cause wobbling of the finished motor. With a one-edged razor blade or sharp scissors start at the center of the circle and snip away small pieces of plastic. Stop when you are about ⅛ inch away from the circle marking. Do not attempt to cut out the entire circle. You cannot do it satisfactorily. You must now use another technique.

Wrap some coarse sandpaper around a broomstick and use this as a file to smooth the hole. Make it as round as you can without going up to the circle. The final rounding will be done on the wand itself.

Wrap about two turns of the sandpaper, rough side facing out, around the wand. Force the cover with its nearly completed circle over the wand and sandpaper. Now rotate the cover or slide it back and forth. The hole will become more and more perfectly circular. Take it off the wand. Remove the sandpaper and test how well the cover rotates on the wand. The movement must be loose, but not too

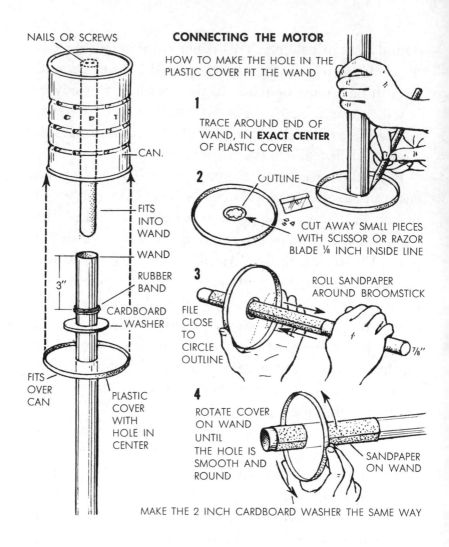

NAILS OR SCREWS

CONNECTING THE MOTOR

HOW TO MAKE THE HOLE IN THE PLASTIC COVER FIT THE WAND

CAN.

FITS INTO WAND

WAND

RUBBER BAND

3″

CARDBOARD WASHER

FITS OVER CAN

PLASTIC COVER WITH HOLE IN CENTER

1

TRACE AROUND END OF WAND, IN **EXACT CENTER** OF PLASTIC COVER

2

OUTLINE

CUT AWAY SMALL PIECES WITH SCISSOR OR RAZOR BLADE ⅛ INCH INSIDE LINE

3

FILE CLOSE TO CIRCLE OUTLINE

ROLL SANDPAPER AROUND BROOMSTICK

⅞″

4

ROTATE COVER ON WAND UNTIL THE HOLE IS SMOOTH AND ROUND

SANDPAPER ON WAND

MAKE THE 2 INCH CARDBOARD WASHER THE SAME WAY

loose. Keep sanding and testing. In short order you will have a hole so precisely round it will surprise you.

When operating the motor, this plastic cover is put over the bottom of the can and the extending end of

50

the wooden shaft. Then the shaft is slipped into the wand. However, if the vacuum cleaner is now turned on, the air will blow the can right out of the wand.

To prevent this, you must place a cardboard washer on the wand *inside* the cover, as shown in the illustration. A rubber band will prevent the washer from moving up the wand. Cut the cardboard ring the way you did the hole in the cover. It is not necessary to be very accurate in this instance.

When setting up the motor, first slip the plastic cover over the wand. Then set the cardboard washer over the cover and about 4 inches from the top of the wand. Wrap a rubber band on the wand above the washer to keep it in place. Set the wooden shaft of the motor into the wand and place the cover over the bottom of the can.

Start the vacuum cleaner, keep the wand vertical, and the motor should turn. For more power, you may have to enlarge the holes in the motor. They should be about 1/4 inch in diameter. You may also make more holes. Try the motor at different depths on the wand by moving the retaining washer. To get a very smooth rotation, place your finger on the center of the top of the can while it is turning.

A carousel turning on top of the can is an amusing sight. Attach a 6–8-inch circular base of cardboard to the can and paste little animal figures on it. It is necessary to use lightweight materials.

INVISIBLE WORDS THROWN INTO AIR

BACK VIEW OF HAND HOLDING BAG

THUD!

SECRETLY SNAP FINGERS THROUGH BAG TO MAKE NOISE

Catching Air in a Paper Bag

This humorous fooler never fails to get everyone's attention. The next time you have an audience, become very serious and remark that you wish to demonstrate a rather curious phenomenon. Everyone knows that air has weight. In fact, 1 cubic foot of the stuff at sea level and at room temperature weighs about 1¼ ounces.

It is also commonly known that when we speak we produce invisible vibrations in the air with the help of our diaphragm, vocal cords, tongue, teeth, and lips. However, it is not generally known that every word we utter is actually a quantity of expelled air. And since air has weight, we should be able to throw words around—and even catch them in a paper bag!

Continue by holding your mouth over your cupped left palm and say a long, funny word, or a series of small words into your open hand. Pretend that you have caught the words. Lower your hand, bend your knees, and move your body from side to side as though you were holding something heavy.

Meanwhile, you are holding in your right hand a large open paper bag (like those used for groceries). Now "throw the words" you hold in your left hand high into the air. Appear to follow the flight of the invisible chunk of air with your eyes. Move the open bag around in an apparent attempt to get under the words as they start falling toward the floor.

Finally, the invisible word falls into the open bag with a loud thud heard by everyone. The bag even makes a downward motion as though something actually fell into it with an impact. This effect catches everyone off-balance. Keep your secret for a while, allowing your friends to ponder over this hoax.

This trick is done by snapping your thumb, which

is not seen by the audience, against the back of the bag. Hold the open bag with your thumb in the back and the index and middle fingers visible in front of the paper. Practice snapping your fingers through the bag so that the action is not seen by the onlookers. If this is done at the same time that the bag is given a downward motion, the illusion is very realistic.

As an encore, pretend that one word got stuck on the ceiling light. Ask everyone to blow at one time to dislodge the word. "Catch" it as it falls into the bag. Pretend to pour the word from the bag back into your mouth. "Conservation, you know!"

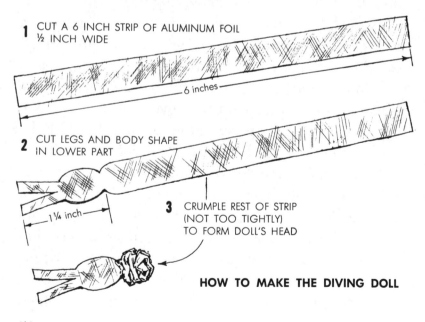

1 CUT A 6 INCH STRIP OF ALUMINUM FOIL ½ INCH WIDE

6 inches

2 CUT LEGS AND BODY SHAPE IN LOWER PART

1¼ inch

3 CRUMPLE REST OF STRIP (NOT TOO TIGHTLY) TO FORM DOLL'S HEAD

HOW TO MAKE THE DIVING DOLL

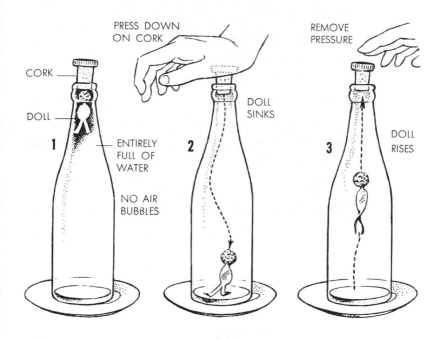

CORK

DOLL

1 ENTIRELY FULL OF WATER

NO AIR BUBBLES

PRESS DOWN ON CORK

DOLL SINKS

2

REMOVE PRESSURE

DOLL RISES

3

Adorable Diving Doll

It is easy to make this tiny aluminum diver. Slip it into a soda bottle that has been filled to the brim with water. By placing your thumb over the bottle opening, you can command the figure to sink or rise quickly or slowly, lie down on the bottom, or stop halfway up.

With scissors, cut a ½-inch by 6-inch strip of aluminum foil (like that used by your mother in the kitchen). Very carefully pinch and shape 5 inches of the foil into a *loose* ball which will be the diver's head, as shown in the illustration. Snip away very small pieces from the remaining inch of foil to complete the diver's body.

Insert the diver into a bottle filled with water. The figure should float, since the head contains trapped air which makes it buoyant. If it does not float, you can loosen some foil or make pin holes in the head. However, it is usually best and quickest to make another diver. This time, do not pinch the aluminum head so tightly and the diver will float.

If necessary, add more water to the bottle until there is a little hill of water above the opening. Place your thumb over the bottle top *so that no outside air is trapped* under it.

Press down hard or easily and the diver starts sinking according to the pressure you exert. Continuous pressure will make the diver reach bottom and lie down. Let up the pressure and the diver will stand on the bottom. Release the pressure, and the diver floats up to the surface.

This historical toy comes in many forms and is called a Cartesian diver. It floats because the trapped air bubbles in the head are large and make the diver buoyant. But when your thumb presses on the top, water (which is not compressible) is forced into the head, making the trapped air bubbles smaller. The diver is now less buoyant and it sinks. Release the pressure, and the compressed air bubbles become larger and force the water out of the head. The diver now becomes more buoyant and floats to the surface.

1 ENTIRELY FULL OF WATER

2 PRESS DOWN WITH THUMB

AVOID LETTING IN AIR BUBBLES

DOLL SINKS

Use showmanship when demonstrating this novelty. For example, you can blow down on your thumb as you press. It will seem as though you are blowing the diver down through the glass bottle! Or suck in your breath, secretly release the pressure, and let the diver come up. Some demonstrators use a magnet and pretend to pull the diver up or down. You might sprinkle "invisible, anti-gravity magical woofle dust" on the bottle to raise the diver.

It should be lots of fun to prepare in advance a diver for each person at a party or club or in a classroom. After your guests play with the divers, tell them that the toys are gifts they may take home. They will appreciate this friendly gesture.

You will have less water spilled if you insert a cork into the bottle top instead of your thumb. Press or loosen the cork to operate the diver.

Another substitute for your thumb is a sheet of rubber from a broken balloon. It is tied to the bottle top with string or with a rubber band. There must be no *air* bubble under the rubber. If you press lightly on the rubber sheet, the diver will sink.

The best kind of diver response is obtained by using a *transparent plastic* bottle with a tight stopper. Fill the bottle so that when the stopper is screwed on tightly there is no air in the bottle. Just squeeze the sides of the bottle between your fingers and the diver will sink immediately.

USE BURNT OUT
MATCH HEAD FOR
EMERGENCY DIVER

Impromptu Cartesian Diver

If you ever find yourself in a group without any aluminum foil, you can make a very obedient Cartesian diver from a paper safety match. Rub the match on the striking surface of a *closed* book of matches. As soon as the chemicals ignite, blow out the flame and stick the match, head up, into the bottle. It will behave like your aluminum ball diver.

The reason for this is that the quickly extinguished match head has holes in it left by the burned chemicals. However, after about 25 sinkings, the paper match (unlike the aluminum ball) may become waterlogged and stay on the bottom.

Identifying Hard-Boiled Eggs

At one time or another, your mother may have had the problem of guessing which eggs in a batch were soft-boiled or hard-boiled. You can show her the scientific trick of determining which is which.

Simply spin an egg on a hard, smooth surface. A hard-boiled egg will spin easily and even rise vertically. A soft-boiled egg will slow down very quickly because of the friction of its loose, liquid contents.

HARD-BOILED   SOFT-BOILED

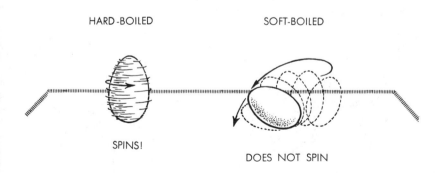

SPINS!

DOES NOT SPIN

This Trick Is a Corker!

Fill a narrow drinking glass with water almost to the top. Place a cork on the water and try to make it stay in the center. You will find it impossible to do since the cork will persistently move to the edge of the glass.

The secret is to slowly add water from another container until the glass is so full that the water surface is actually above the rim. Carefully drop the cork in the center and it will now stay there.

The surface of the water acts like an elastic membrane and takes this curved shape without running over. This is due to the attraction that water molecules have for each other, a phenomenon called SURFACE TENSION.

The highest part of this "pulled-together" surface film of water is in the center. The cork therefore floats to this high spot.

Do this trick near the sink or over a large soup plate.

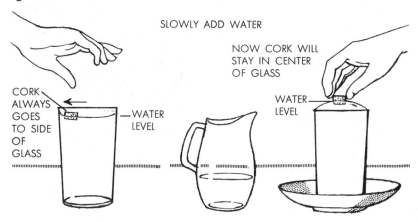

SLOWLY ADD WATER

NOW CORK WILL STAY IN CENTER OF GLASS

CORK ALWAYS GOES TO SIDE OF GLASS

—WATER LEVEL

WATER LEVEL

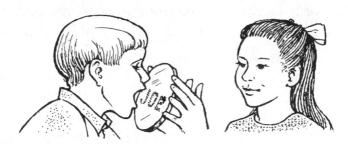

A Personal Test for Life

One of the classical tests used by doctors and other people to see whether a person is alive is to hold a cool mirror very close to the mouth. Condensation forming on the mirror is a sure sign of life. It shows that the person is undergoing a living process called oxidation. In this case the hydrogen in the body cells and elsewhere is combining with oxygen. The chemical reaction produces hydrogen oxide, which is water.

Tell the friend you wish to test whether he is really alive or simply a walking zombie. Hold a mirror *close to his mouth.* Call attention to the mirror's clarity by asking him to look at himself. Now ask him to huff very hard on the mirror until the mirror is completely fogged over.

To the person's amazement, not only is he proved to be alive, but his own name appears in the midst of the tiny, condensed water droplets. Yet he will swear that it was not there before the test.

To prepare for this trick clean a pocket mirror or vanity mirror or use a section of window. Write the initials or name of the person on the glass with the corner of a soap eraser or the eraser on the end of a pencil. Since the letters are still visible, you must use a handkerchief or soft cloth to waft or gently brush away the excess rubber. Hold the cloth very, very lightly. After *a few passes* over the letters you should not be able to see any sign of them. Condensation does not take place where the invisible layer of rubber is located.

The breath is usually warmer than the mirror so that fogging will occur every time. However, the best results are obtained when the mirror or glass is cool. Keep the mirror near the window in the winter or in a refrigerator for a while in the summer.

Instead of initials you may have other secret messages appear. When removing writing from a mirror, you must use soap or detergent, otherwise the letters persist on the glass.

You can try another method of writing the letters. Make a weak solution of detergent and water. Wet the tip of your finger and write your message on the glass. If it is still visible when it dries, brush it very gently until you can hardly see it.

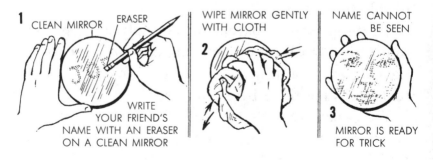

1 CLEAN MIRROR ERASER
WRITE YOUR FRIEND'S NAME WITH AN ERASER ON A CLEAN MIRROR

2 WIPE MIRROR GENTLY WITH CLOTH

3 NAME CANNOT BE SEEN
MIRROR IS READY FOR TRICK

The Dissolving Coin

This trick will completely confuse your friends because it is based upon several deceptions utilizing scientific principles.   Ask a person what happened, and
he will say that he dropped a half-dollar into a glass
of water.   He heard the click as the coin fell.   Yet
the coin disappeared—even when the water was
poured out of the upturned glass.

Like all good tricks, this one calls for a few minutes
of simple practice.   You will also need several unusual, but easily acquired objects.   Here is how this
trick is done.   Show your friend the half-dollar and
say that you are going to drop it into the water.   On

second thought, you will allow him to do this. You place a handkerchief over the coin and let him hold the money through the cloth and over the glass.

However, under cover of the handkerchief you have secretly substituted a round piece of window glass the size of the coin you now have hidden in your palm. Your friend thinks he is holding the half-dollar. Remove your hand so that the palmed coin cannot be seen; put the coin into your pocket and quickly remove your hand. However, leave the coin in the pocket when you remove your hand. Pretend you went to your pocket to get some magic "woofle dust." Sprinkle some of this invisible dust over the handkerchief.

Instruct the person holding the coin to drop it into the water when you count to 3. Slowly say 1, 2, 3, raising your voice at 3. When the "coin" is dropped, get an end of the handkerchief and shake it out to show there is nothing left in it. At this point pick up the glass. Say that water, whose chemical formula is H_2O or HOH is one of the mightiest dissolvers known to man. It even dissolved the metal coin. . . .

Pour the water from the glass into the sink or another container. Turn the glass upside down while pouring. Then set the glass upright again. This ends the stunt.

The round piece of window glass is about the size of a half-dollar. It is obtained from the front of a very old, useless flashlight you may still have in your

64

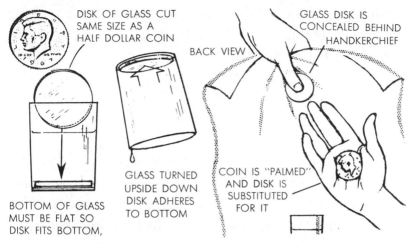

DISK OF GLASS CUT SAME SIZE AS A HALF DOLLAR COIN

BACK VIEW

GLASS DISK IS CONCEALED BEHIND HANDKERCHIEF

GLASS TURNED UPSIDE DOWN DISK ADHERES TO BOTTOM

BOTTOM OF GLASS MUST BE FLAT SO DISK FITS BOTTOM,

COIN IS "PALMED" AND DISK IS SUBSTITUTED FOR IT

house. (Modern flashlights use round pieces of plastic to protect the bulb.)

If you cannot find an old flashlight case, you can easily acquire a suitable circle of glass by going to your local glazier or glass repairman. He has a circular glass cutter which can be adjusted down to the size of your coin (half-dollar or quarter).

Ask him to please cut a few circles from a piece of scrap glass. He probably will not charge you for these, especially when you tell him why you need them. Most automobile glass shops use these circular cutters all the time and have them set up on stands and easily available.

Now look around your home for a drinking glass whose bottom is the same or very close to the size of your glass circle. This is usually a short wine or cocktail glass having slanted sides. If you do not possess such a glass at home, go to a dime store or similar open-counter store with your glass circle. Try it on the glasses in which you think the circles will fit. You will certainly find an inexpensive glass which you can use for the trick.

When water is in the proper drinking glass, the glass disk is invisible when it fits over the bottom. That is because water and glass are almost identical optically.

When the water is poured out, the flat glass adheres (sticks) to the bottom of the glass. Even when the glass is turned upside down, air pressure and adhesion will prevent the glass circle from loosening and falling out. If the piece of glass is the same size as the glass bottom your friend may examine the drinking glass. He will not see the disk.

To work perfectly, the drinking glass *must* have a flat bottom. You will find that some unsuitable glasses have slightly rounded bottoms inside. If you cannot find the drinking glass you need, you may use a clear or opaque plastic glass or even a tin can. A small can in which frozen orange juice is sold is good. But, of course, then you cannot let the person look into the can after the trick. So after you pour out the water, replace the can right side up on something above eye level.

When presenting this fascinating trick, use a heavy handkerchief, colored bandanna, or cloth napkin which is not transparent. Start off by innocently holding the glass disk *behind* the handkerchief alongside your body. Practice placing the handkerchief over the drinking glass while positioning the glass circle under your fingers in the center of the cloth and palming the real coin. Practice until every movement seems natural.

Never tell your friend what you are going to do *before* you do it. Do not say that the water will dissolve the coin until you have the real coin firmly hidden away in your pocket. As a magician, you must never tell everything that you are going to do, for then everyone would be on the alert and would question your every action. But if you do everything, including the secret move, in a natural manner, you will not be watched so closely.

When dropping the glass disk, adjust your friend's hand so that he drops the glass at a slant. It will fall faster and cause a louder click. When dropped flat, the glass is cushioned by the big surface of water. However, you may wish to call the number 3 so loudly that it will drown the sound of the dropping coin.

Done properly, this trick will bewilder even your clever friends. That is why it pays to spend a little time preparing for it.

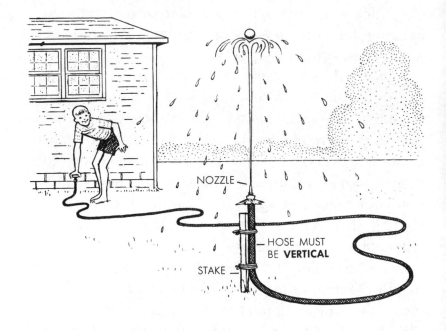

NOZZLE

HOSE MUST BE **VERTICAL**

STAKE

Dancing Ping-Pong Ball

A favorite spectacular target at a shooting gallery is a small ball gaily bouncing up and down on a vertical jet of water. The ball magically remains on top of the stream of water for the same reason (explained on pp. 37–9) the balloon stayed inside the blowing air stream of a vacuum cleaner.

This stunt is done out of doors with a garden hose and a ping-pong ball. The full stream of water is not suitable, so you will have to produce a jet. Remove the rubber from one end of a medicine dropper. Insert the nozzle part of the dropper through the center of an 8-inch square of strong plastic cut from a bag or other substance.

Draw some of the pierced plastic around the medicine dropper and wrap a rubber band tightly around the joint. Now tie the rest of the plastic securely around the open end of the hose with some cord, as shown in the illustration.

The medicine-dropper tube should be in the center of the hose opening and pointing in the same direction as the hose. Open the water valve a trifle and you should have an excellent jet. WARNING: Too much water pressure may burst the plastic.

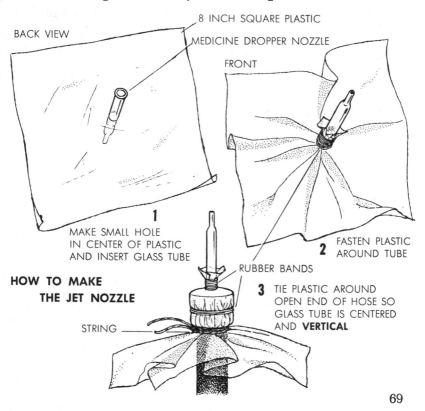

8 INCH SQUARE PLASTIC

BACK VIEW

MEDICINE DROPPER NOZZLE

FRONT

1

MAKE SMALL HOLE
IN CENTER OF PLASTIC
AND INSERT GLASS TUBE

2 FASTEN PLASTIC
AROUND TUBE

**HOW TO MAKE
THE JET NOZZLE**

RUBBER BANDS

3 TIE PLASTIC AROUND
OPEN END OF HOSE SO
GLASS TUBE IS CENTERED
AND **VERTICAL**

STRING

Arrange some means of holding the hose and its jet-producing device in a vertical manner. Tie the hose to some vertical object such as a stake in the ground. Use your ingenuity with whatever you have available, but the jet *must be vertical*. Adjust the hose so that the falling water comes close to or right over the nozzle.

Make a small jet about 2–3 feet high and place the ping-pong ball on top of the stream. It will dance about, but it will not easily fall off unless there is a wind blowing it.

For real fun, slowly turn the water valve so that the stream gets higher. See how far you can bring the ball. Now don't be selfish and play with this for hours—give your friends a chance too!

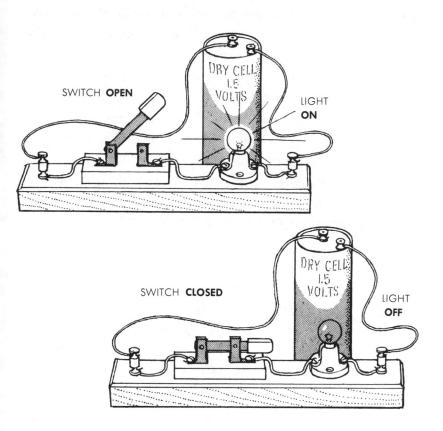

The Impossible Circuit

Here is an electrical trick which will make everyone sit up and take notice. No one will believe it when they see it, because it defies everything they have been taught. It will bewilder your friends and parents and offer many puzzling moments to your science teachers—and even engineers.

It consists of a simple electric light circuit on a

piece of wood. There are two binding posts for connecting a 1½-volt dry cell, and also a porcelain knife switch and a miniature porcelain socket containing a 1½-volt bulb. The clearly exposed wiring is apparently hooked up correctly.

The fascinating feature of this elementary circuit is that the bulb is glowing brightly *while the switch is open*. But when you close the knife switch, *the light goes off*. Just the opposite of what should occur.

Even if your smart friends suspect that things are not what they seem, they will have difficulty in designing a circuit which will give these results. Hand them a pencil and paper and let them try. Do not give them the answer until they solve the puzzle themselves or beg for the solution.

The secret is that the very innocent-looking circuit is a fraud from beginning to end. There is hidden wiring underneath the switch and the socket and also under one terminal. When the knife switch is open, the concealed wiring completes the circuit to the bulb. When the switch is closed, the light goes off because the closing of the knife switch *has caused a short circuit*.

Look at the illustration showing the side view and also the secret bottom wiring. When a 1½-volt dry cell is connected to terminals 1 and 6, the bulb lights up with the switch open. This is because the bulb is receiving current directly from terminal 6 and also from terminal 1 through the hidden wire from 2 to 4.

72

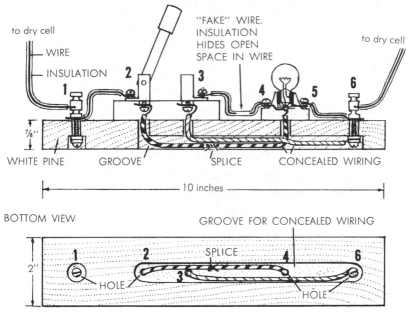

SIDE VIEW, SHOWING WIRING

to dry cell

WIRE

INSULATION

"FAKE" WIRE.
INSULATION
HIDES OPEN
SPACE IN WIRE

to dry cell

1 2 3 4 5 6

7/8"

WHITE PINE   GROOVE   SPLICE   CONCEALED WIRING

10 inches

BOTTOM VIEW   GROOVE FOR CONCEALED WIRING

2"

1   2   SPLICE   4   6

HOLE   3   HOLE

When the switch is closed, the light goes off because of a short circuit caused by the hidden wire from 3 to 6. In other words, it is the same as connecting both dry-cell terminals to each other.

The wooden base is a piece of white pine about 7/8 inch thick, about 10 inches long and 2 inches wide. Arrange the binding posts, knife switch, and socket in a straight line exactly as illustrated. Drill holes for the binding-post bolts. Use a counter-sink or a large drill, or cut away the wood on the bottom of these holes so that the bolt heads are slightly recessed from the bottom of the wood. Also make a small hole through the wood under each of the two contacts of

73

the knife switch. Make another small hole under the center of the miniature socket.

If you do not have a drill, you can make suitable holes by piercing the wood with a red-hot nail held by a pair of pliers. Carefully heat the nail in the gas-range flame. Do this while your parent or some older person is present.

Make a ¼-inch groove on the bottom of the wood from hole 2 to hole 6. If you drill the holes in a straight line, the groove will pass through all the holes. Carefully gouge out the grooves with a pointed knife or chisel. A screwdriver may be used as a chisel here if you gently tap it with a suitable object such as a piece of wood, rather than a hammer, so as not to mar the handle.

The bottom of the knife switch has two screws which hold the top metal contacts. Attach a 6-inch length of insulated wire to each screw. Of course, remove the insulation where the wire goes under the screw head. Now examine the bottom of the socket. There is probably a hard material resembling sealing wax there. Scrape this away with an awl or nail. You will find an exposed brass strip running from one connecting screw outside the socket to the center of the bulb contact. Attach a length of wire to the strip by loosening the screw in the *center* of the socket. Put the bare end of your wire under the strip and then tighten the screw again. If you loosen the screw too far during this operation and the strip falls off, it is a simple task to reassemble the bottom of the

74

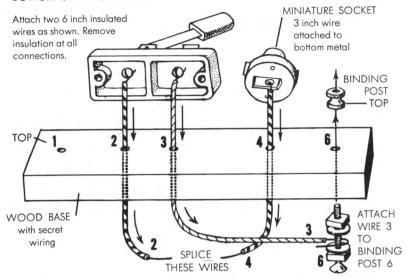

Attach two 6 inch insulated wires as shown. Remove insulation at all connections.

MINIATURE SOCKET
3 inch wire attached to bottom metal

BINDING POST TOP

TOP

WOOD BASE with secret wiring

SPLICE THESE WIRES

ATTACH WIRE 3 TO BINDING POST 6

socket. If you still have difficulty, you may have to solder the wire to the strip.

In assembling the parts, draw the two wires from the switch down through the holes you made in the wood and lay them in the groove. Splice the number-2 wire from the switch to the number-4 wire going to the center of the socket. The number-3 wire is connected to the end terminal as shown. Bend all the wires so that they stay in the groove. Both wires must be insulated from each other. The groove can be filled with plastic wood or other filler. Sandpaper the bottom until it is smooth and paste a strip of felt over the entire bottom to hide the deception.

Another way of hiding the bottom wires and groove is to attach the circuit board to a larger base. Then, of course, there is no need to fill in the groove.

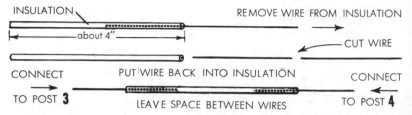

Neatly wire the top with insulated wire. Use the kind whose plastic insulation can be pulled off the wire and then slipped on again. This is necessary because the short length of wire between 3 and 4 is a fake. It is actually a broken wire. Make it by pulling out the copper wire from the insulation, cutting it in half, and carefully replacing the two wires into the insulation. Leave a small gap between the wires. No one will suspect the deception. This wire must be broken. If it were whole, there would be a permanent "short" in the circuit. Make sure the broken ends do not touch under the insulation.

When demonstrating the puzzle, do not keep the switch lever down for more than a brief time, since continuous short circuits consume dry cells quickly. When your friends keep the knife switch down during their contemplation, simply open the switch in a matter-of-fact manner. It may bother some of your expert friends that you have to short-circuit a dry cell to demonstrate this puzzle. However, in this case, where you are using only 1½ volts and bell wire, it is perfectly safe to have momentary shorts. Dry cells used intelligently with this electrical trick have lasted for months.

Doodling with a Rubber Band

Mysterious Heat Production
Tightly stretch a rubber band held between your two
hands and quickly touch it to your lips. Suddenly
loosen it, and again touch it to your lips. Repeat the
stretching and loosening. Keep placing the rubber
band against your nose, ear tips, forehead, and cheek
after each *sudden* stretching or loosening.

Pretty soon, the friends near you will swarm over,
full of curiosity. Without answering any questions
about your apparently foolish behavior, hand each
one a rubber band. Like monkeys, everyone will
begin imitating you.

It may take a little while, depending upon the
sharpness of your buddies, but someone is finally

going to shout, "Hey, the rubber gets hot when it's stretched, and cool when it's loosened!" Soon everyone will be delighted to also discover this startling fact. And so ends an interesting lesson in psychology and science.

Use rubber bands which are about ¼ inch or more in thickness so that there will be no breakage. Scientists are not quite sure why stretching rubber produces heat, or why loosening pulled rubber makes it cool. Perhaps the heat is due to the increased collisions and friction of the rubber molecules when they are stretched and under tension. Some scientists think there is a similarity between stretching a rubber band and compressing gas molecules. In each case, heat is produced, and then when pressure is released there is a cooling effect.

From personal experimentation you and your friends will no doubt discover that your lips are very sensitive to heat. More so than the other spots on the face which were tested. That is why a mother will sometimes place her lips against her sick child's forehead to feel whether he has a high temperature.

Finger tips have a great many nerves in them compared to other parts of the body. Are they very sensitive to heat as well as to touch? Place one end of the rubber band between your teeth or on some kind of hook and pull it with one hand. Place the fingers of your free hand on the stretched rubber. Are your finger tips more sensitive to heat than your lips?

78

Puzzling Expansion of Rubber

Everyone knows that almost all materials get larger when they are heated and smaller when they are cooled. People become highly skeptical when you tell them that a stretched rubber band behaves in an opposite manner. It *contracts* when you heat it and *expands* again when cooled. You can prove it by demonstrating this attention-getting expansion meter, easily constructed from simple materials.

Use a rubber band which is ¼ inch wide and about 3½ inches in length. Stretch it around the sides, from top to bottom, of a quart-size milk carton. If the pouring end of the carton is not the flat kind, cut the top, making flaps which can be folded flat. Turn the container upside-down so that the smooth bottom is now the top.

Obtain a round toothpick and a 10-inch length of thin wire (22 gauge or less) which will be the instrument's pointer. Leave an inch of wire at the start for leverage and wind about six very tight loops around the end of the toothpick. The wire must bite into the wood so that it will turn when the toothpick turns.

Slip the middle of the toothpick under the center of the rubber band. Snip off any excess wire so that the pointer clears the table. Mark off a dial face on the milk carton or paste one on. Adjust the wire pointer so it is in the center of your scale.

Illustrate the action of the meter for your friends by pinching the rubber band on one side of the tooth-

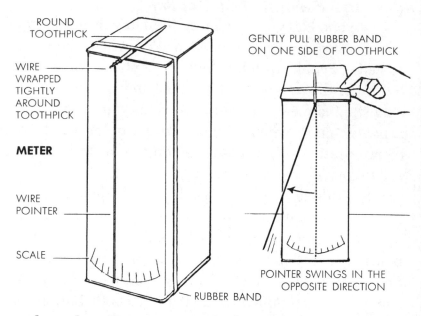

ROUND TOOTHPICK

WIRE WRAPPED TIGHTLY AROUND TOOTHPICK

METER

WIRE POINTER

SCALE

RUBBER BAND

GENTLY PULL RUBBER BAND ON ONE SIDE OF TOOTHPICK

POINTER SWINGS IN THE OPPOSITE DIRECTION

pick and pulling it toward the side of the carton. The pointer will swing in the opposite direction. Make sure everyone understands that this is what should happen whenever that portion of the rubber band contracts. Again adjust the pointer so that it is in the center of the scale and does not scrape against the container.

Carefully light a safety match on a *closed* book of matches. Hold the burning match over the top of the rubber band, on one side of the toothpick. The rubber band will contract and make the toothpick with its pointer turn. This tiny movement is magnified into a larger movement by means of the large arc made at the end of the wire. The tip of the pointer should move from 1–2 inches. Watch the indicator move back again when the rubber cools and expands.

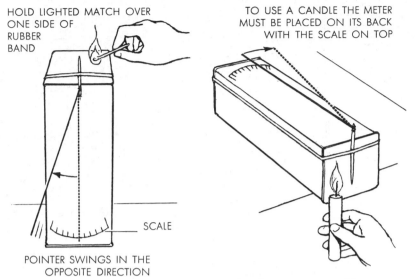

HOLD LIGHTED MATCH OVER ONE SIDE OF RUBBER BAND

TO USE A CANDLE THE METER MUST BE PLACED ON ITS BACK WITH THE SCALE ON TOP

SCALE

POINTER SWINGS IN THE OPPOSITE DIRECTION

There should be no draft in the room. Do not scorch the rubber band. It is not necessary to get too close with the match. To avoid having to strike many matches on the cover, have a lighted candle in a nearby saucer to ignite the matches.

You cannot use a candle instead of matches to heat the rubber band when the meter is in an upright position. A slanted candle will drip wax over the rubber. If you wish to use a candle, set the meter on its back with the scale facing up. Of course, not as many people will be able to see the scale in this position. Adjust the wire by pulling it upward so that it does not scrape against the carton.

Raise the meter on something so that the flame from a vertical candle can get close enough to heat the rubber. A cigarette lighter may also be used, but remember that if you get too close and overheat the rubber band it will snap, because it is under tension.

81

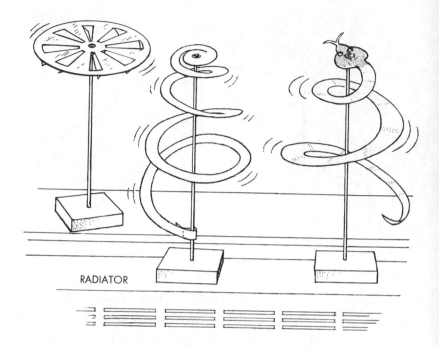

RADIATOR

Colorful Whirligigs

There is something particularly merry and festive about having several colorful spinning devices continuously operating in your home. They are easy and interesting to make from cardboard, drawing, or construction paper. Sturdy whirligigs can also be built from aluminum foil or thin aluminum pie plates.

You have a wide choice of types of spinners. Each kind becomes a gay conversation piece, especially if you use colored paper or foil. You may also paint your own masterpiece with the help of easily applied watercolor.

These rotating scientific toys work because of rising currents of warmed air. They can be placed on or above radiators, hot-air registers, or other moderate-heat devices. They can also be made fireproof by utilizing aluminum or copper foil. Then they may be mounted over kitchen stoves, fireplaces, lighted candles, or electric lights, or even over the ventilation slits of hot television sets.

One of the most fascinating eye-catchers is a lively spiral snake you can cut from paper or foil. Use tracing or carbon paper to transfer the spiral in the illustration to the material you decide to use. Carefully cut along the lines.

The dot in the center represents the pivot. Make a small dot there with a sharp pencil. Insert one half of a small dress snap into the hole and snap on the other half. Because of the tiny cup in the snap, your spiral will spin with very little friction over the pointed end of your stand.

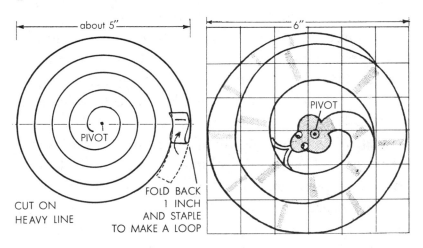

about 5″

CUT ON
HEAVY LINE

FOLD BACK
1 INCH
AND STAPLE
TO MAKE A LOOP

PIVOT

6″

PIVOT

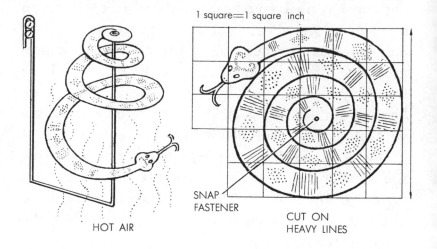

1 square=1 square inch

SNAP
FASTENER

HOT AIR

CUT ON
HEAVY LINES

You may obtain dress snaps from old garments discarded by your mother or sister or you may use new ones. If you do not have any available at the moment, simply make a pointed dent in the paper—but do *not* pierce it. Place this depression over your pointed stand. However, if you use a dress snap, the spiral will stay on its pivot more securely.

A simple stand is a long knitting needle pierced through a large cork or tightly stuck into a hole drilled into the center of a 3-inch square block of wood. A large spool can also be made to serve as a base.

Instead of a knitting needle, you may use a length of wire cut from a wire clotheshanger. File the top end to a point and bend the bottom so it can be nailed or screwed to a block of wood. Another stand is a long sharp pencil, or a thin flagstick or dowel pointed in a pencil sharpener. Whatever you use,

84

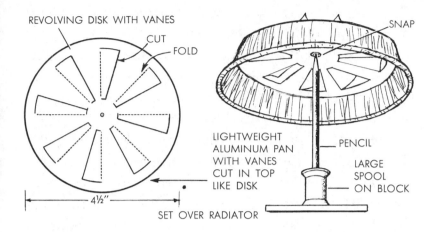

REVOLVING DISK WITH VANES
CUT
FOLD

SNAP

LIGHTWEIGHT
ALUMINUM PAN
WITH VANES
CUT IN TOP
LIKE DISK

PENCIL

LARGE
SPOOL
ON BLOCK

4½"

SET OVER RADIATOR

make the base sturdy so that it does not tip over. You may wish to place the stand a short distance *above* the heat source. Then you will have to bend a length of wire from a hanger into the necessary shape. Point one end and attach the other end of the wire to the woodwork using screws or string or even by resting it under a weight such as a book on a shelf.

You can make a spiral spin in the opposite direction by turning it inside out. In other words, reverse the dress snap and turn the spiral upside-down. For added interest place a few spirals which are moving in opposite directions next to each other.

The bottom of the spiral may be too long. Then it will become too sluggish or it will touch the base. Cut a section off the end and fashion a new snake head.

Sometimes the spiral moves too fast, or for some

other reason will get outside the vertical stand. A good remedy is to wrap the bottom of the spiral loosely around the vertical wire and staple the paper to itself so that the loop does not come apart. Fast-moving aluminum spirals placed over stoves often move extremely fast and it becomes necessary to make a retaining loop on the bottom.

There are also many other types of whirling devices in addition to the spirals. Keep your eyes open for them. Some are sold in hardware stores for about ten or fifteen cents. They are used over warm electric lights and in artificial fireplaces for producing special effects. Toy counters in dime stores often have toys containing twirlers, for example, the whirling tails of toy birds or the spinners carried by children on sticks. Of course, you can also make or buy propellers.

These are moved by the wind but they will also turn when mounted to catch the rising hot-air currents. Examine them and then make your own models if possible. Display a collection of various kinds in suitable locations in your home or school. The illustrations show you several other kinds you will have fun making. Use a compass, scissors, or single-edged razor blade.

Just imagine what a colorful and exciting display you can have with 20 models whirling madly at one time!

Skinny Printing

Hand someone a card containing a maze of very closely ruled parallel lines. Your friend will not know what to make of it. Then say that the card contains a message, but one must first learn to read it. After some manipulation and viewing the card from all angles, your experimenting friend will suddenly grasp the secret. It is intriguing that the printing can become so clear when it was completely unintelligible a few moments before.

It is just a matter of perspective. When the card is held so that one eye looks along the flat side of the card, the parallel lines suddenly become printed letters and numbers.

THE SKINNY ALPHABET

Look at the illustrated alphabet and numerals to get the general idea. Then get a ruler and a very sharp pencil or pen and practice making the letters. In a short time you will become an expert and then spend many fun-filled hours amusing your friends.

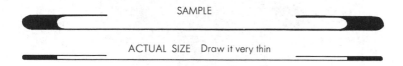

SAMPLE

ACTUAL SIZE   Draw it very thin

You should aim to make letters which cannot be distinguished when read normally. You will be surprised at how closely your lines can be drawn and yet be readable. Use a card with a smooth surface. The backs of most business calling cards are suitable. Make the letters the long way.

It is also possible to draw lines at right angles across other lines. When held properly, the printing in each direction can be read very clearly.

Fooling Around with Numbers

Mathematics and science go hand in hand. So while you are doing some scientific magic it will improve your image as an entertainer to throw in some unusual tricks dealing with numbers. Your audience will often get additional pleasure if they are also given the clever mathematical explanation for the trick.

For good visibility, the numbers may be written with chalk on a blackboard. If this is not available, use black crayon on a large piece of blank paper taped to a door or wall.

Lightning Addition

You can demonstrate your prowess as a mathematical genius by adding five rows of five-digit numbers in a twinkling of an eye. And, if you wish, you can introduce many magical predictions because you always know the answer in advance. Here is the basic idea:

Tell your friends you are going to do something with five-digit numbers. Ask for such a number. Put it on the board, or have someone else do the writing. Call for another number and place it under the first number. Then quickly give and write the third number. Once again, someone calls out a number which is jotted down. Make up the last number to be added. Quickly draw a line under the rows to be added, and turn toward the audience.

Ask how long it should take for a person to add the five numbers. After getting several estimates, say that you have already obtained the answer. Turn around, and quick as a flash write the sum where it is normally written. Have your friends laboriously check your addition.

Suppose these were the numbers used:

     24,736 (someone gave this number)
     48,621 (someone also gave this)
     51,378 (you offered this)
     13,942 (this was given)
     86,057 (you gave this number)
   224,734 total

You probably will not see it right away, but the sum is actually obtained from the top number. To get the sum you must place a 2 in front of the top number and subtract 2 from the top number. Also notice that the numbers you gave for lines 3 and 5 always added up to 9 with the numeral above it. In other words, lines 2 and 3 add up to 99,999 and lines 4 and 5 also give 99,999. Learn to do this with no hesitation in your presentation.

This is all you need to know to do this trick. However, if you are one of those curious people who likes to know the reason for the behavior of numbers, here is what is happening.

In reality you are adding two rows of 9's to your key number. The sum of these rows is 199,998; this is 2 less than 200,000:

$$
\begin{array}{r}
99,999 \\
99,999 \\
\hline
199,998
\end{array}
$$

So, if you place a 2 to the left of your five-digit key number, you are adding 200,000. But you only wish to add 199,998—so you subtract 2 on the right.

Amazing Predictions

Now that you know the bare bones of the trick, you are in a position to produce spectacular variations. For example, as soon as anyone writes the first number you really know the answer. At this point, show a blank envelope and a blank sheet of paper. Write a number on the paper. Do not tell anyone what you wrote or why-you did it. Suspend the sealed envelope from a string overhead, or tack it to something nearby in full view of your friends, or let someone hold it while standing at your side. After the trick is done, have someone open the envelope and read the predicted number. Have this done with much fanfare and showmanship.

For a real "miracle," try this trick. Get your hands on a dollar bill whose serial number starts with 2. The trick is to have your column of numbers add up to the serial number on the dollar bill. Needless to say, you either "plant" the bill on someone in the audience or give it to someone who is your assistant. Then, for the end of the trick, you can ask him to read the first six digits of a dollar he "may have in his pocket." You can do the same with a person's automobile license—if there is a 2 before the serial number. Here's an idea of how to work the trick.

If the first six digits of the "planted" dollar bill are 278,436, then your top number of the list of numbers to be added must be 78,438. You get this by omitting the 2 from the left side of the serial number and now *adding* 2 to the right digit. This top number is called off by one of the friends who are helping you. You may also pretend to read the number from a bill you remove from your wallet. No doubt, you can think of more clever means of introducing this necessary key number.

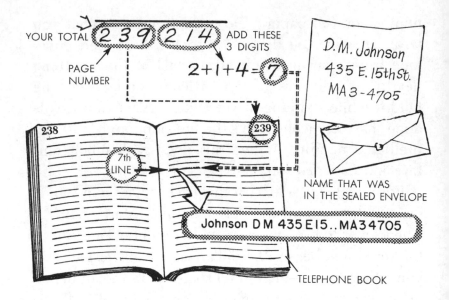

YOUR TOTAL 2 3 9 2 1 4 — ADD THESE 3 DIGITS

PAGE NUMBER

$2+1+4=7$

D. M. Johnson
435 E. 15th St.
MA 3-4705

238   239

7th LINE

NAME THAT WAS IN THE SEALED ENVELOPE

Johnson D M 435 E15..MA34705

TELEPHONE BOOK

Telephone-Book Predictions

Another variation of the fast addition trick is this one. The trick is to obtain a sum of numbers tied into a hidden name from the local telephone book. It will seem as though the sum were obtained by chance from the audience. Of course, you will have your assistant in the audience give you the key number.

Here is how it's done. Place in a sealed envelope the name of a total stranger with his address and telephone number. As we will see, this "happens to be" the same information in the local telephone book on the page and line indicated in the trick. Suppose the sum is 239,214.

Review with the people that this sum was obtained by chance from numbers given by the audience. It will now be used to indicate what is printed on a certain page and line in the directory. Explain that you will do this in the following manner. Put a circle around the sum's first three digits, 239. This is the page in the directory. To obtain the line, say that you must add the last three digits in the sum; 2 plus 1 plus 4. The sum, 7, is the line on the selected page. Use only the first column to the left on page 239, and go down to line 7. Have someone read or write the information from the telephone book. Compare it with the information in the sealed envelope. With good presentation and patter this effect is startling.

Confusing the Smart Ones

In order to throw your brighter friends off the track, and make it more difficult for them to get leads to the solution, here are several variations. Do not have the key number on the top. Let it be in the second row, the first number being one called off by a person in the audience. Let the third number add up to 9's with the first number. When the fourth number is given, have it put all the way up on top. The last number will be down below. Do not lose track of your key row.

You can see how this routine will prevent having dangerous telltale lines of figures next to each other. The issue may be further clouded by having others (secretly helping you) call off the numbers which you ordinarily would give to add up to 9's.

As you can see, there are endless variations to this apparently simple trick. You can work it up so that it acquires professional showmanship.

A *Perplexing Mathematical Stunt*

Another amusing trick with numbers can be performed for an individual or for many people at the same time. Each person will need a pencil and a blank sheet of writing paper. At the end of a simple exercise in arithmetic, everyone will be left delighted —but absolutely flabbergasted at the outcome.

Ask everyone to:

    a. write down the number of his house
    b. double this number
    c. add 5
    d. multiply by fifty
    e. add one's age
    f. add the number of days in a year (365)
    g. subtract 615

This is the end. Your friends now examine their own results which, of course, are different from all the others. Tell them that the last two numbers on the right represent their age. The other numbers to the left will be each person's own home address.

This is the basic trick. If you repeat it as given above you will always get the person's own house number on the left, and the age on the right of the final arithmetic answer.

The explanation of this confusing stunt is that your friends are asked to perform certain mathematical operations whose results cancel each other out. This leaves the original numbers, such as the addresses and ages which were not canceled. As you can see, the cancellations are done very deceptively.

Since you are a modern student, you have probably already studied very simple algebra. You should be able to understand what is happening as we follow the a–g instructions for performing the trick:

a. let H represent your home address
b. double it and get 2H
c. add 5; the result is 2H + 5
d. multiply this by 50 and obtain (2H + 5) 50
e. add *age;* this gives you (2H + 5) 50 + *age*
f. and g. add 365; subtract 615 and the entire operation now looks like this:

(2H + 5) 50 + *age* + 365 — 615

Remove the parentheses by multiplying everything inside it by 50.

100H + 250 + *age* + 365 — 615

Now you can clearly see how the numbers cancel each other, since +250, +365, and —615 is zero!

So your final number is

100H + *age*

The purpose of multiplying your house number by 2 and then by 50 was to actually multiply it by 100. This means that the number is beyond the unit's or the tenth's place. It cannot interfere with your age. Isn't this clever?

Introducing Novel Variations

Your friends' confusion will be greater if you repeat the trick, this time changing the conditions. Instead of beginning with the house number, use any other number which has a special meaning.

Such figures may be the numbers on the family car's license plate, omitting the letters. Library-card numbers may be used, or the year the person was born, and even the first half-dozen figures on a dollar bill.

Instead of the age in step (e) ask for the amount of change in one's pocket. Remember that this amount of money must be less than one dollar. If it is more, it will run into the hundred's place and interfere with the number on the left. In fact, any number you use here instead of the age must have only two digits.

Substitution of any number for house number or age does not call for any other changes in the a–g routine. As long as 365 days are used, you simply ask to have 615 subtracted at the end. Incidentally, before you say 615 you should hesitate and pretend to be silently calculating this figure.

Now suppose you wish to use some other number instead of 365 days of the year. For example, at step (f) people may be told to add the number of their school or the number of the month and year or some other figure. If you do this, then you must tell the person to subtract a number other than 615. This you can easily calculate.

Another way, suppose that when you come to step (f) you look at the clock and say, "Let us all add the time at this very moment." If the time is 2:30, then everyone adds 230.

Of course, for step (g) you cannot say that everyone should subtract 615 since 615 is used to cancel 365 + 250. The figure 250 cannot be changed. Do your own calculating to see what number you get when you add the basic 250 to whatever number you introduced. In this case it was the time, 2:30. Add 230 to 250 and you get 480. To cancel this number, you must tell everyone to subtract 480.

The rule, then, is to *add whatever number you introduce in step (f) to 250.* This sum is the number which people must subtract in step (g), the end of the trick. After a while you will become so familiar with the routine that you will easily make up endless variations, tailor-made for your audience. Everyone will call you a mathematical wizard!

```
B O E y J b D R E e
M A E r E H U T I n
J U N r O N e e S C
I R N O g a n L A g
2 A P F C P A A I O
R t n E S 9 M A I N
A T A T A U I T N U
L A C m e S m R C H
N D s J d A A N R d
M p A B Y L U e O e
```

Creating Secret Messages

You are certain to stir up much mystery and amusement when you mail your friend a daily secret message on a postal card. Of course, the family will be able to see this open correspondence and will go mad trying to make sense of the letters. However, even the F.B.I. or the decoding experts in the Pentagon will have difficulty cracking this puzzling cipher.

Look at the square of jumbled letters in the illustration. You cannot unlock the secret of their meaning unless you have a key. In this case, in order to read individual words, you must have a card which is ruled off into small squares. Some of these small squares have been cut away. This allows letters to be seen when the perforated card is placed over the jumbled printing.

After the card is placed into position 1 (with the 1 in the upper left corner), and the visible letters are read, it is turned so that the 2 is in the upper left corner. Each time the card is rotated, new words can be read. As you can understand, turning the card also makes it extremely difficult for someone to figure out how to cut another card like the one you are using.

There are 144 evenly ruled squares on the card, twelve squares on each side. Because the card will be rotated in different positions, its four sides must be perfectly square. If you wish to make a small 3-inch card which will allow messages to fit on postal cards, you must have ¼-inch squares. The graph paper used in mathematics is suitable. To stiffen the graph paper, carefully glue it to a square sheet of cardboard.

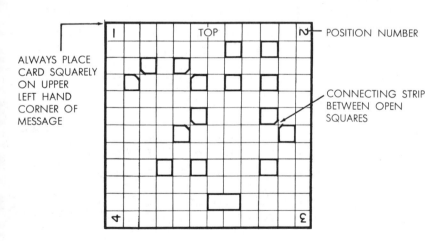

For greater comfort and ease of manipulation, it is better to make a larger card about 4⅝ inches square. This will contain ⅜-inch squares. Start from the square-cut corner of a sheet of cardboard or stiff paper. Since the lines on most ruled writing papers are ⅜ inch apart you can use them for laying off points on each of the four edges. Then carefully rule off the squares.

Use the card in the illustration as a model. Count how far each perforated square is from the edges in the model. Verify your count and then mark the squares on your own cipher to be cut out. Use a single-edged razor blade. Protect the table with an old magazine or layers of paper. Notice that squares which are diagonally next to each other have a small connecting strip as reinforcement. These are made by piercing with the corner of the razor blade.

Mark off the position number in each of the corners and print the word TOP. When using the cipher, always square up each position of the card with the upper left-hand corner of the paper on which you are writing the message.

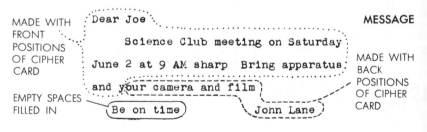

MADE WITH FRONT POSITIONS OF CIPHER CARD

EMPTY SPACES FILLED IN

MESSAGE

MADE WITH BACK POSITIONS OF CIPHER CARD

Dear Joe

Science Club meeting on Saturday June 2 at 9 AM sharp Bring apparatus and your camera and film

Be on time   John Lane

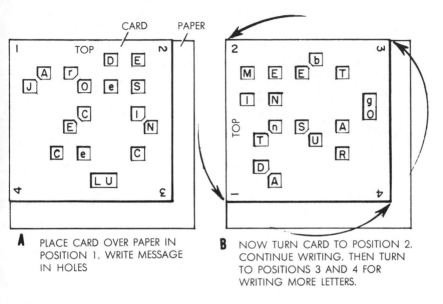

A PLACE CARD OVER PAPER IN POSITION 1. WRITE MESSAGE IN HOLES

B NOW TURN CARD TO POSITION 2. CONTINUE WRITING. THEN TURN TO POSITIONS 3 AND 4 FOR WRITING MORE LETTERS.

Print capital letters in the center of each open space, proceeding along each line from left to right. When the last open space in position 1 is filled, simply turn the card to position 2, etc. To make it easy to see the end of one word and the beginning of the next one, do not capitalize the last letter of each word. However, this is not necessary. If you wish you may mark an "X" as a spacer.

You can print a total of 68 letters using the front of the card in all four positions. If you turn the card over, you will have four more positions; 5, 6, 7, and 8. Put a circle around the six squares shown in the rear illustration. Use the circled openings to continue your message. In this way you will be able to include 24 more letters.

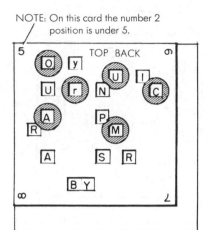

NOTE: On this card the number 2 position is under 5.

5   TOP BACK   6

8   7

C FOR POSITIONS 5, 6, 7, 8
TURN CARD OVER. WRITE ONLY
IN CIRCLED SQUARES,

REMOVE CARD

```
    O E y   J b D R E
M A E r   E H U T I n
J U N r O N e e S C
I R N   g a   L A g
2 A P F C P A A I O
R t n E S 9 M A I N
A T A   A U   T N U
L A C m e S m R C H
N D s J d A A N R d
p A B Y L U e O
```

D FILL IN ALL BLANK SPACES
WITH ANY LETTERS.

Remove the card when you are finished and fill in every blank space in the jumbled square of letters. Use any letters as fillers. Of course, if your message does not use the full capacity of this cipher, you may stop at any point. Then fill in the blank spaces with meaningless letters.

You may wish to use more letters for messages than you can obtain from the front and back of your card. In this case, after position 8, continue writing your message without the card by filling in all the blank spaces in the regular order. You will now be utilizing every available spot for 100 letters.

However, it will be impossible to read the message composed of the additional letters, since there is no card to pick them out from the jumble of letters. To remedy this, the reader must make a check next to every letter read through the card. Then he will be able to read the unchecked letters which were added without the card.

Make several cards so you can send secret messages to many friends. Perhaps this may start you off on a new and fascinating hobby called cryptography. This is the art of writing in secret codes. There are many books in the library for young readers on this topic.

This study is considered very important by our government. Many excellent mathematicians are employed for deciphering codes. Computers and code-breaking machines are used to help the experts.

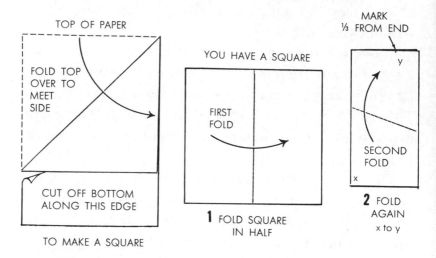

Making a Five-Pointed Star with One Snip!

A wonderful talent for scientists and engineers to possess is the ability to get a clear mental image of the final appearance of something that is undergoing an alteration or change in shape. See how good you or your friends are by practicing with this brain-teasing puzzle.

Can you fold a sheet of paper so that when you make one cut with the scissors you will produce a reasonably perfect five-pointed star?

Start off with a square piece of scrap paper. You can obtain a square of any size without using a ruler as follows. Use a sheet having two parallel sides and

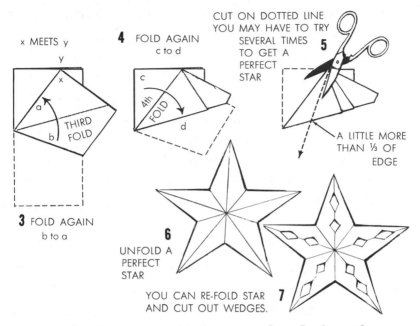

x MEETS y

4 FOLD AGAIN
c to d

CUT ON DOTTED LINE
YOU MAY HAVE TO TRY
SEVERAL TIMES
TO GET A
PERFECT
STAR

5

THIRD FOLD

4th FOLD

A LITTLE MORE
THAN ⅓ OF
EDGE

3 FOLD AGAIN
b to a

6
UNFOLD A
PERFECT
STAR

YOU CAN RE-FOLD STAR **7**
AND CUT OUT WEDGES.

a squared-off top. Fold the top edge flush with any side, as shown in the illustration. Fold the bottom of the triangle you formed. Cut or tear along the fold. Open the paper and you will have a square.

To make the star, fold your square in half, then fold it in angles. After each trial, make one cut with the scissors. Observe what you did wrong, then try again and again. You will find yourself getting closer to the solution each time. But if you finally have to give up because "insanity" is closing in, then study the illustrations carefully.

Practice until you can make a perfect star each time. These stars are excellent for party decorations. Make them from tinted aluminum or other metallic

107

foil, or just colored construction paper. If you use white drawing paper, you may wish to paint the stars in many hues and designs with watercolor.

Compare your stars with a similar sized, perfect geometric star easily made with a compass as illustrated. First make a circle. Now increase the radius of the compass so that it is about another sixth of a radius longer. Start at any point on the circle and lay off five small arcs. Your fifth arc should be right over your starting point. If not, you must increase or decrease your radius very slightly until your five arcs come out even. You can do this in several trials.

Use a ruler and pencil to connect the points where the arcs cut the circumference as illustrated. You will see a perfect five-pointed star.

If you wish some added fun, you may refold your star and cut wedges or other designs on the folds. When the star is opened you will discover five diamond-shaped holes for each wedge you cut.

MAKING A FIVE-POINTED STAR WITH COMPASS AND RULER

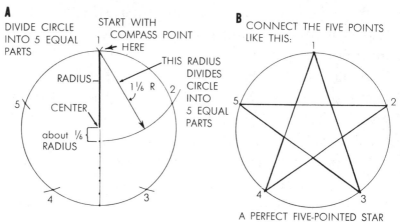

A PERFECT FIVE-POINTED STAR

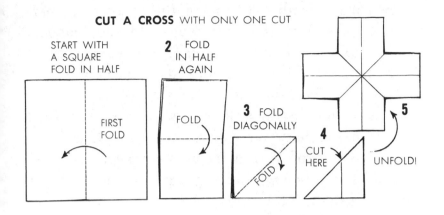

START WITH
A SQUARE
FOLD IN HALF

FIRST
FOLD

2 FOLD
IN HALF
AGAIN

FOLD

3 FOLD
DIAGONALLY

FOLD

4 CUT
HERE

5

UNFOLD!

Cross-Cutting Pastimes

Now that you and your friends are in a party mood and the table is littered with paper snips, you may wish to follow up the star-cutting exercises. This time try making crosses, also with one cut of the shears.

This is much easier and should give all the frustrated star-makers a chance to regain their self-respect. Almost everyone can follow in their minds what is going on behind the folds. Those who cannot, alas, will probably never become candidates for engineering degrees.

Start with a square sheet of paper. Fold it in half, and again fold the long side in half. This leaves you with a smaller square one-quarter of the original size. Now fold along the diagonal so that all the other folded ones are together.

The bottom of your triangle should have all the open edges. With one snip of the scissors cut perpendicularly from the open edges to the diagonal fold. Open the folds and you should have a cross. The thickness of the cross depends upon how closely you cut parallel to the folded edges.

This method produces a cross with every leg equal in length. Should you wish to cut a religious cross, you must start off with a rectangular piece of paper. A good size is one whose length is one and a half or two times the width.

Follow the simple instructions in the illustration. If you vary the final cut so that it is closer or farther from the folded edge, you will obtain a thinner or a thicker cross.

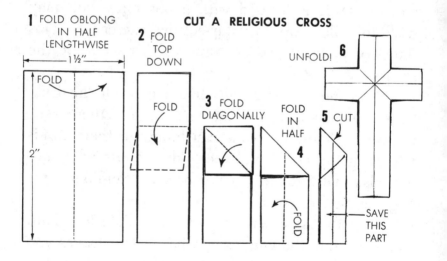

1 FOLD OBLONG IN HALF LENGTHWISE

CUT A RELIGIOUS CROSS

2 FOLD TOP DOWN

UNFOLD! 6

3 FOLD DIAGONALLY

FOLD IN HALF

5 CUT

4

SAVE THIS PART

Walking Through a Calling Card

Show your friends an ordinary business card carried by salespeople. Ask if anyone can walk right through this small card. If you get no sensible response, prod them with the following hint. They may cut up the card in any way they see fit in order to make a very large hole.

The chances are that very few people can visualize the type of cuts needed to produce the accordion pleats shown in the illustration. When everyone gives up, show them a duplicate card which you have prepared.

Carefully open the slits which you have made with a single-edged razor blade. You will form a circle large enough to place over a person's head and through which he can step.

In preparing the card, first rule the lines with a sharp pencil. Draw the lines as close as you can. With a little practice you can prepare cards strong enough to be handled and yet have slits $\frac{1}{16}$ inch apart.

Try various grades of cards, including playing cards. Some have considerable strength even when sliced into very thin pleats. Do your cutting over a smooth piece of wood or a sheet of heavy cardboard.

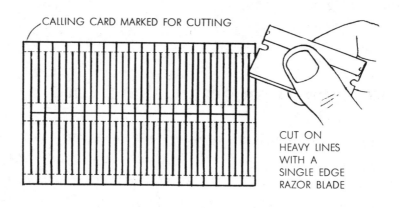

CALLING CARD MARKED FOR CUTTING

CUT ON
HEAVY LINES
WITH A
SINGLE EDGE
RAZOR BLADE

The Unthinkable Peg

This extraordinary puzzle is a favorite brain teaser of an inspiring science teacher. Every term he introduces it to his classes and science club for the purpose of stimulating imaginations. First he passes around several pieces of wood, each one containing three differently shaped, cut-out openings—a circle, a triangle, and a square.

He then demonstrates how a wooden, circular cylinder or a sphere can fit exactly into the round hole.

A small triangular block fits snugly into the next opening, and a third block just fits the remaining hole. Then he poses this question: "Instead of using the three separate blocks, who can visualize, draw, or make a clay model of just *one* single block which will fit perfectly into all 3 holes?"

He hands out scrap paper and soft modeling clay and soon the room is buzzing with mental and manual activity. Quizzical brows are furrowed, and many models are made and remade until the first successful experimenter whoops "Eureka! I've got it!"

When you construct this absorbing puzzle to keep among your scientific oddities, it will soon become your favorite conversation piece. The instructions given here are for models made of wood. However, many excellent ones have utilized cardboard, clay, and soapstone. If you are good at soap carving you might even try this material.

As you can see in the illustration, the peg which fits all three holes is a round cylindrical piece of wood with two slanted sides. First obtain a round piece of wood from a ⅞-inch dowel or an old broom or mop stick. An old window-shade roller is excellent to use because it is made of very soft wood and is extremely easy to file or sandpaper.

You may also use a piece of round poling on which the hangers are suspended in a clothes closet. Of course, this would make a much larger peg than one ⅞ inch wide. But no matter what size you have avail-

MAKING THE WOODEN PEG

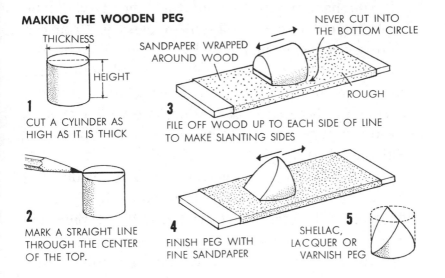

1 CUT A CYLINDER AS HIGH AS IT IS THICK

THICKNESS
HEIGHT

2 MARK A STRAIGHT LINE THROUGH THE CENTER OF THE TOP.

3 FILE OFF WOOD UP TO EACH SIDE OF LINE TO MAKE SLANTING SIDES

SANDPAPER WRAPPED AROUND WOOD

NEVER CUT INTO THE BOTTOM CIRCLE

ROUGH

4 FINISH PEG WITH FINE SANDPAPER

5 SHELLAC, LACQUER OR VARNISH PEG

able and decide to use, cut the peg so that its height is exactly equal to the thickness. In this way it will fit exactly into a square hole. Keep this fact constantly in mind.

To make the two slanted sides which form the triangle, first draw a straight line (diameter) through the center of the top of the peg. Very carefully start planing or filing to form a slanted side. When working, never remove any wood beyond the drawn line on top and never go into the bottom. When the peg is done, the round base *must* remain intact as a circle. Slant the other side in the same manner. Keep examining your work and constantly making corrections. The slants must be exactly opposite each other.

115

If you have a vise to hold the peg, it would be helpful but it is not absolutely necessary. You can improvise a good filing tool by wrapping sandpaper around a flat stick, like a ruler. Start off with coarse sandpaper and end with a finer grade. Another scheme is to lay a sheet of sandpaper on a flat surface. Grasp the peg in your fingers and scrape it back and forth on the sandpaper.

The block with the three holes may be made from ½-inch or ¾-inch wood. Drill the round hole with an auger bit. The other holes are cut with a coping saw or file. If you do not have the proper tools for working with wood, you may cut the three openings from cardboard. Discarded cardboard advertising posters may be obtained from your friendly druggist. This material is extremely durable. Lay out the dimen-

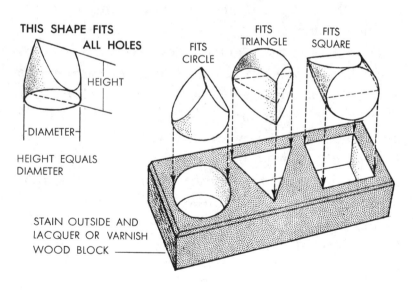

THIS SHAPE FITS ALL HOLES

HEIGHT

DIAMETER

HEIGHT EQUALS DIAMETER

FITS CIRCLE

FITS TRIANGLE

FITS SQUARE

STAIN OUTSIDE AND LACQUER OR VARNISH WOOD BLOCK

sions carefully, depending on the size of the peg used.

When demonstrating the solution to the puzzle, grasp the slanted ends of the peg and insert the circular base into the round hole toward your audience. Everyone can now see how perfectly the peg fits the circular opening. Now insert the triangular side of the peg into the triangular hole. When showing how the square fits, you should have the circular base down, and one slanted side facing you.

Wax, lacquer, shellac, or varnish the peg. For a beautiful two-tone finish, first carefully shellac only the inside of the three holes. Avoid getting shellac on any other part of the unpainted wood. When the shellac is dry, use a dark stain on the rest of the wood. Any stain which gets on the shellac can be easily wiped off.

Riddles, Jokes, and Such

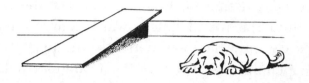

Why is an inclined plane like a lazy dog?

Answer: An inclined plane is a slope up (slow pup). A slow pup is a lazy dog.

.   .   .   .   .

A woman was having a house designed for her by an architect. He asked her which of the four sides of the building she would like the builder to face toward the south. She innocently replied that she would be very happy if all sides could have a southern exposure.

She was told that this was indeed possible, but she would not like to live in such a house. Why not?

Answer: Such a house would have to be built right on the North Pole. At that frigid location, *every* direction is south.

A racing yacht is anchored offshore. A rope ladder hangs over the side so that the bottom rung touches the water. There are ten rungs which are 1 foot apart. The tide is rising at the rate of 1 foot an hour. Which rung from the bottom will be touching the water at the end of 2 hours?

Answer: The bottom rung will still touch the water, because the entire yacht remains at the same depth regardless of the tide.

. . . . .

If an athlete gets athlete's foot, and an astronaut gets missiletoe (mistletoe), what does a surveyor get?

Answer: Square feet.

. . . . .

How can you make figures lie?

Answer: Write the number 317 and read it upside-down. It spells LIE.

119

How would you pronounce GHOTI?   It is a cold-blooded animal.

Answer: GHOTI may be pronounced FISH.   It is used by English professors to show how illogical our language must often sound to a foreigner.   The gh is pronounced as in "cough"; the o as in "women"; the ti as in "nation."

• • • • •

Can you read this word?

Answer: The white letters "THE" are on a black background.   Once you see the word, you will wonder how you ever missed it.

Can you write 1,000 without picking up your pencil from the paper?

Answer:

Bend over the edge of a sheet of paper and make the following continuous, curved lines on both the flap and the page.

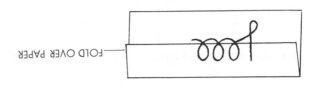

FOLD OVER PAPER

.   .   .   .   .

How can two people stand on a sheet of newspaper face to face without being able to touch each other?

Answer:

Place the sheet under a doorway and let each person stand on it on either side of the door.

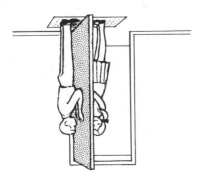

Some people are foolish enough to wish to be rocketed to the moon for their vacations. What will they have to purchase from their travel agents?

Answer: Lunatickets!

. . . . .

Look at this picture. What do you see?

Answer: Most persons at first will see a white urn in a dark background. Others see the profiles of two people facing each other.

Can you arrange four 9's so that the total is 100?

Answer: $99\frac{9}{9}$

. . . . .

Alas! The thirsty freshman
He isn't any more.
For what he thought was H_2O
Was H_2SO_4.

Index